THE **CATECHISM** IN A **YEAR**

COMPANION

VOLUME I: DAYS 1-120

Fr. Mike Schmitz
Petroc Willey
Ann Koshute

ASCENSION
West Chester, PA

Ascension
PO Box 1990
West Chester, PA 19380
1-800-376-0520
ascensionpress.com

Cover design: Teresa Ranck

Printed in the United States of America

23 24 25 26 27 5 4 3 2 1

ISBN 978-1-954882-18-8 (trade book)
ISBN 978-1-954882-19-5 (e-book)

Dedicated to the 2023 listeners of
The Catechism in a Year (with Fr. Mike Schmitz)™

Thank you for being the first group to journey through the *Catechism of the Catholic Church* with us. Your thoughts, questions, and feedback inspired this book.

We are praying for you—please pray for us, and we cannot wait to see you tomorrow.

CONTENTS

INTRODUCTION

If you journeyed with us through *The Bible in a Year*, you learned the story of salvation. A part of that story is how God revealed his incredible love for us slowly, over the course of centuries. The fullness of God's revelation was when he sent his only begotten Son, Jesus Christ, into the world to preach the Good News of salvation.

As we know, after his ascension the Lord sent out the Holy Spirit upon the apostles, and they immediately began to spread the story of God's love to everyone they met—and then throughout the world. The Acts of the Apostles tells the story of this beginning of the Church.

While the book of Acts ends after twenty-eight chapters, we know that the story of the Church has continued. For the past two thousand years, Christians have brought the Gospel of Jesus Christ to a world hungry to know God. At first, the apostles preached to those who were raised in the faith of Abraham, the people of Israel, whose story is told in the Old Testament. Soon after, St. Paul and others began preaching the Gospel to those who did not know anything about God's covenant in the Old Testament.

Early on, the Church had to develop a comprehensive and intelligible way to communicate the Faith to people who were hearing about the one true God for the first time. In the early centuries of the Church, it often took people three years to learn the Faith. Someone's entire worldview needed to be re-shaped and re-fashioned. Many had to learn that God was one, and that he was good and just. They needed to learn that Jesus cared about them—and even loved them to the point of giving up his own life so that they could have life. Many had to learn of the dignity of the human person. Because of this, the process of becoming Christian did not just involve a transfer of *information* but an actual *transformation*.

The *Catechism of the Catholic Church* is more than just information about the Catholic Faith. It is more than just bits of data about what we believe about God, about the world, and about the human person. The *Catechism* is a blueprint for life. Its first part, or pillar, by presenting the Creed, tells us what we believe about God, revelation, faith, the human person, and our eternal destiny with God. But it then seeks to lead us to a place of conversion, to a place of love. This first part of the *Catechism* seeks to tell us who God is to lead us to love him. After all, how can we love what we do not know?

As you go through this first volume of the *Catechism in a Year Companion*, keep in mind that what you are listening to is the result of the Gospel being proclaimed for two millennia to people just like you. You are in good company. All who have gone before us were called to a conversion of heart, to love God with their whole heart, mind, soul, and strength; they were called to be saints—and so are you.

–Fr. Mike Schmitz

Note: This book is based on *The Catechism in a Year (with Fr. Mike Schmitz)* podcast.

HOW TO USE THIS *CATECHISM* IN A *YEAR* COMPANION

This *Catechism in a Year Companion* provides a number of ways to help you live your life in the fullness of the Catholic Faith. In this first volume, you will be guided through days 1–120 of the podcast by three features: **Reflect on the Faith**, **Take It to Prayer**, and **Dive Deeper**.

- **Reflect on the Faith** is a summary of Fr. Mike's commentary on the readings for that day. These are important points to remember and key takeaways as you are learning.
- In **Take It to Prayer**, you will pray along with Fr. Mike every day, using a transcript of the prayer he prays in the podcast. Read it aloud as you listen, repeat it throughout the day, or pray it before you go to sleep.
- Each day, you will be given an opportunity to **Dive Deeper** into the *Catechism*. Sometimes this section will include an *image* of a key element or event mentioned in the *Catechism* or an *answer* to a frequently asked question about the readings. Some days, it might be a *prayer prompt* to use during your prayer time or a *challenge* to live out what you have heard in your life.

In addition, **introductions** to the four parts of the *Catechism* are included in these *Companions*. Here, Dr. Petroc Willey explains the significance of the part's color coding, notes its key teachings, and presents a breakdown of its sections and chapters. At the end of each period, Dr. Willey offers a **review**, including a short recap of what has been discussed and review questions to help you recognize how much you learned.

INTRODUCTION TO PART ONE

THE **BREAKDOWN**

This first part of the *Catechism* is about what we believe. It proclaims who God is and his intention in creating us. It conveys the great sweep of his plan of love—of what he has done and continues to do for us. The very first paragraph of the *Catechism* gives us a summary of this plan of God.

Part 1 is divided into a section about divine revelation and a section about the Creed.

Section 1 prepares us to learn about God's plan of love by setting out for us *why we can know it is true*: God has made us with every capacity to know and long for life with him (chapter 1); he has made sure that his loving plan is communicated securely to us (chapter 2); and he gives us everything we need to share in his life and entrust ourselves to him (chapter 3).

Section 2 *outlines God's plan* in the narrative form provided by the Creeds, from the beginning of Creation to the fulfillment of all things in everlasting life. This section is divided for our convenience into three chapters corresponding to the three Persons of the Holy Trinity. At the same time, it is also divided into twelve articles representing the twelve apostles, for whom the Apostles' Creed is named.

KEY **TEACHINGS**

The first part of the *Catechism* is all about God—his actions, his love, and his intentions. How we need to respond to God comes later, in the third and fourth parts of the *Catechism*. At the heart of part 1, then, is the Church's teaching on God himself—a Trinity of Persons in a communion of love. The teaching on the Trinity, Father, Son, and Holy Spirit, enlightens how we read and understand everything—every doctrine in this part expresses who God is and helps us learn more about him and love him more deeply.

Reflect on the **Faith**

- In these first two days, we are reading the Prologue of the *Catechism*.
- We are going to talk about what God's plan for human beings is. The very first paragraph in the entire *Catechism* begins by talking about the revelation of God to humanity.
- "God, infinitely perfect and blessed in himself, in a plan of sheer goodness freely created man to make him share in his own blessed life. For this reason, at every time and in every place, God draws close to man" (CCC 1).
- God "calls man to seek him" (CCC 1). We know that every time we seek the Lord, that is actually a response to his offer of grace.
- Everyone who is a disciple of Jesus is called to pass on the Faith. How do we hand on the Faith from generation to generation? First, "by professing the Faith"—by sharing it with words—second, "by living it in fraternal sharing," and third and fourth, "by celebrating it in liturgy and prayer" (CCC 3).
- What is God's plan for you and for me? His plan is for us to know him and to share intimately in his life. Because we know that, we are moved by love of God to share it with everyone we meet in whatever way we can.

Take It to **Prayer**

Father in heaven, we give you praise and thanks. You have made us. You have made us for yourself. And we are restless. Our hearts are restless until they rest in you. God, what is your plan for us? What is your plan for each of us this day? Lord, we open our hearts to you today and open our minds to you. God, remove any sense of intimidation. Remove any sense of fear. Remove any sense of even resistance to what it is that you have revealed in your Scriptures and through the teachings of your Church for these past two thousand years. Open our hearts and our minds today as we begin this journey. So that, again, without fear, without resistance, without any hesitation, we can just launch ourselves into your arms today. What is it that you want for us? What is it you want from us? And what is it that you can do in us this day if we just open our minds and open our hearts to you? Lord, reveal the answer to this. Reveal yourself to us. In Jesus' name, we pray, Amen.

Dive **Deeper**

ST. AUGUSTINE

This image shows St. Augustine contemplating the truth of God with heart aflame. It is the very knowledge of God he learns from Scripture that inspires divine love. We are made, like St. Augustine, to know and love God (see CCC 1).

Reflect on the **Faith**

- The *Roman Catechism* (1566) of the Council of Trent was a response to the challenging questions that arose during the Protestant Reformation. The *Catechism of the Catholic Church* (1992) was issued to express the eternal truths of the Faith in a more up-to-date way.
- The *Catechism* is built on four parts, or "pillars: the baptismal profession of faith (the *Creed*), the sacraments of faith, the life of faith (the *Commandments*), and the prayer of the believer (the *Lord's Prayer*)" (CCC 13).
- The four parts of the *Catechism* are about these four pillars.
- The *Catechism* was written first for bishops and those who teach in their name—priests and catechists. But the *Catechism* notes that it will be helpful for all Catholics to read it, and that includes us. (See CCC 12.)
- The *Catechism* includes references to Scripture, excerpts from Church documents, and quotes from saints and liturgical material. (Much of this is referenced in the footnotes and is not highlighted on the podcast; it can be seen in the text of any recent edition of the *Catechism*.) This is a way to highlight the fact that the whole Faith is united.
- When we teach the Faith, we have to consider the people who are listening.
- The *Catechism* is not fuel to win arguments. As the *Roman Catechism* says, "The whole concern of doctrine and its teaching must be directed to the love that never ends" (CCC 25). This is the love of God himself.
- Jeremiah 31; Daniel 14; Proverbs 16:21-24

Take It to **Prayer**

Father in heaven, we give you praise, and we thank you so much. Thank you so much for bringing us to this day. We ask you to please give light to our eyes, that we can see your goodness. Open our ears, that we can hear your truth. And open our hearts, that we can be transformed by your goodness and transformed by your truth. We make this prayer in the mighty name of Jesus Christ, our Lord. Amen.

Dive **Deeper**

What are all the abbreviations that are in the *Catechism*? What is the difference between a Scripture citation with a "cf" and one without?

The *Catechism of the Catholic Church* is a rich and accessible guide to the teachings of the Church. But it is not a comprehensive encyclopedia of all that has been said and written over the centuries leading to a deeper understanding of the Faith. References are included in the *Catechism* to give readers some context for the teachings presented and to allow for further reading and personal study. The Index lists the abbreviations of the sources used in the *Catechism*, such as ecclesiastical documents (for example, papal encyclicals and decrees of Church councils) and Scripture. When a passage of the Bible is simply referred to rather than quoted directly, the abbreviation "cf." (short for "confer," meaning "see") is used. For scholars, the *Catechism*'s many references and footnotes provide context for a particular paragraph or teaching. For all the faithful, they are an invitation to enter more deeply into the teachings of the Church and grow in greater intimacy with God. (Note: See the Introduction beginning on page 1 of the *Catechism of the Catholic Church*, Ascension Edition to find out more about the sources within the *Catechism*.)

Reflect on the **Faith**

- The *Catechism* is more than knowledge. It is an invitation to a relationship, and God is calling us to intimacy.
- The first pillar, the Creed, speaks of our quest for God, who is wooing us and calling us. It puts everybody on an equal playing field and gives us three ways that we can know something of God.
- First, we can know something about God through creation. We can look at creation, the laws of the universe, and the stars, and know that there is a creator.
- Second, our very longing for God tells us that there is a God.
- Finally, we can come to know something of God through reason.
- God reveals himself in Scripture, in words and deeds. Divine revelation teaches us what we could not otherwise learn for ourselves through creation, our own nature, or reason.
- God also reveals himself in Sacred Tradition.
- The deposit of faith has been handed on from one generation to the next from the apostles through their successors, the bishops. They are charged to keep the Faith and teach it completely, without adding to it or subtracting from it.
- In this first pillar, "What We Believe," we learn about this revelation, and we are prepared to respond to God. The name the Church gives that is the obedience of faith.
- This obedience of faith is not mere "believism." While it consists of intellectual assent, it also means personally entrusting ourselves to the truth.
- We do not just want to pass on data. Faith is about conversion of heart. It is not just getting to know the one who has created and redeemed us, but also being drawn more deeply into relationship with him. It is not just *information* but *transformation*.

Take It to **Prayer**

Father in heaven, we give you praise and glory. Thank you for bringing us to day 3. Thank you for bringing us to this place where we can learn more about you, where we can know your identity and know our deepest identity as your beloved creation, as those who have been adopted by you in Baptism and made into your sons and your daughters. Help us to know you as our Father. Help us to know you, God, as Father, Son, and Holy Spirit and be drawn into your love. This day, we ask you to please bless this conversation. Bless Jeff, bless me, and please bless everyone who is listening to us today. In Jesus' name, we pray. Amen.

Dive **Deeper**

Think of a time in your life when you felt a longing for God in your heart. Do you desire to be drawn more deeply into relationship with him? Entrust yourself to God today and orient your intentions toward growing in intimacy with him.

Reflect on the **Faith**

- God loves you. Most people do not truly believe this; they believe that God merely tolerates them. But God loves every person he has created.
- You and I do not have to exist. But we *do* exist. The reason you and I exist is because God wants us to exist. God loved us into existence.
- We can be indifferent to God's love.
- In seeking God, we need four things: (1) we have to *think*; (2) we cannot be fickle; (3) we must do what we believe to be right; and (4) we need the example of people leading us to God (see CCC 30).
- The *Catechism* states that we can come to know God through creation and human beings. We can look at the world around us, and we can conclude that God exists. Beauty in the world points to the beauty of the artist, the Creator of this world.
- The human person has a "sense of moral goodness," is free, and desires to be happy (CCC 33). As C. S. Lewis said, "Creatures are not born with desires unless satisfaction for those desires exists. A baby feels hunger: well, there is such a thing as food. A duckling wants to swim: well, there is such a thing as water ... If I find in myself a desire which no experience in this world can satisfy, the most probable explanation is that I was made for another world."[1] We crave God, and that craving means we can realize that there is such a thing as God.

Take It to **Prayer**

Father in heaven, you have made us for yourself, and our hearts are restless until they rest in you. Inflame that desire that we have to know you. Inflame the desire that we have to be found by you. And inflame that desire that we have to find you. You reveal your heart to us. Help us to reveal our hearts to you. Help us not to be numb to the reality that you are. And help us not to be numb to the reality that you are love. We make this prayer in the mighty name of Jesus Christ, our Lord. Amen.

Dive **Deeper**

Praise God for loving you into existence! Praise him for the beauty of his creation and the desire he has placed in you to know him! In prayer, recognize God's presence and abundant love from a humble heart of gratitude and awe for his sheer goodness.

Reflect on the **Faith**

- We can come to a knowledge of God's existence "by the natural light of human reason" (CCC 36).
- While we can apprehend that God truly exists and even understand a bit of who God really is, we are limited in what we can know. This is one of the reasons why God has to reach out and reveal himself to us.
- In Romans chapter 1, St. Paul says that even those who have never heard of the living and true God will still experience the consequences of rejecting him. (See Romans 1:18–23.) This is because they have the light of human reason and can look at the world around them. Our human capacity for understanding allows us to know in a certain sense not only that God exists but who he is.
- In the encyclical *Humani Generis*, written by Pope Pius XII in 1950, the pope talks about how the knowledge of God "call[s] for self-surrender and abnegation" (quoted in CCC 37). When I come to know that God is, then it means: *Oh, I'm not God.*
- Sometimes, even if we know something is true, we can imagine it to be false. As Pope Pius XII teaches, "The human mind ... is hampered ... by the impact of the senses and the imagination, but also by disordered appetites which are the consequences of original sin." We can readily tell ourselves that something we do not wish to believe "is false or at least doubtful" (quoted in CCC 37).
- Even though he has revealed himself to us, even though we recognize we have received the fullness of the revelation of God, all "our human words always fall short of the mystery of God" (CCC 42).

Take It to **Prayer**

Father in heaven, we give you praise. You are "the inexpressible, the incomprehensible, the invisible, the ungraspable" (CCC 42). You are a mystery. You are the mystery of mysteries. And yet, you reveal your heart to us. You reveal your identity to us in the world you created, in the human heart that beats inside every one of our chests, in our minds. Everything you created, Lord, in some way points to you, our Creator. Help us to get rid of all those things that get in the way. Help us to overcome those obstacles that can make it difficult to see you, or difficult to acknowledge your goodness. And open our hearts. Open our minds to not only love and understand you but also to let you love us. In Jesus' name, we pray. Amen.

Dive **Deeper**

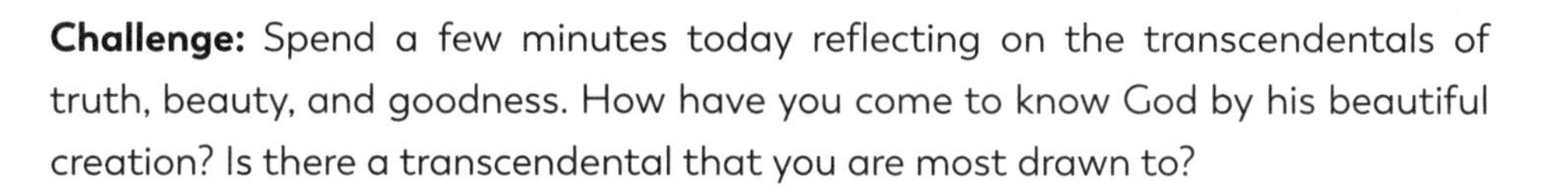

Challenge: Spend a few minutes today reflecting on the transcendentals of truth, beauty, and goodness. How have you come to know God by his beautiful creation? Is there a transcendental that you are most drawn to?

Reflect on the **Faith**

- A human being is a body-and-soul composite. We are animals who live on this earth, but we are also spiritual beings called to have communion with God.
- The very fact that you exist reveals that God wanted you to exist, which means he loves you. He does not have to love you, but he chose to love you when he chose to create you. You are alive on purpose.
- We can live a fully human life only if we freely live by our bond with God.
- Living a life of faith does not mean that the circumstances and situations of our daily lives will not have tragedies, trials, and sorrow. But when we are completely united with God himself, our lives are complete.
- One of the most pervasive myths that has been put forth by our culture is that faith and science are opposed to each other. But they cannot be opposed because truth can never contradict truth. Faith asks about *supernatural* realities, and science asks about *natural* realities.
- One of the things that marks modern human life is a crisis in meaning. If this world is accidental, nothing has ultimate meaning and our lives only have a subjective value.
- But we believe that human beings, and this world, were brought into being by an objective Creator, who had a purpose for creating this universe and a purpose for creating you and me.

Take It to **Prayer**

Father in heaven, we give you praise. We ask you to please open our minds, open our hearts to receive your truth. Open our hearts to not only hear what is true about you, but to really allow the truth to change us. Because, Lord God, you are true. You are the Truth. And when we apprehend you, when we grasp you, when you grasp us, you set us free. Because you are the God who gives life, and you give liberty. But you give life and liberty through this paradoxical step of self-surrender. And we surrender ourselves to you. This is when we experience true freedom. This is when we experience true joy. This is when we experience what it is to live. So, Lord, please help us to live today. In your name, we pray. Amen.

Dive **Deeper**

You came from love, were created by love, and are made for love. In prayer, reach out to God with confidence in this truth. Ask for the strength to direct your life toward him, who is a love that never ends.

Reflect on the **Faith**

- As St. Irenaeus of Lyons writes, "The Word of God dwelt in man and became the Son of man in order to accustom man to perceive God and to accustom God to dwell in man, according to the Father's pleasure" (quoted in CCC 53).
- We can look at God's creation and get to know something about God. But if he wants us to know his heart, then he is going to have to reveal himself.
- As the Baltimore Catechism says, God made us to know him, to love him, and to serve him in this life so as to be happy with him forever in the next.
- "By revealing himself God wishes to make ... [human beings] capable of responding to him, and of knowing him, and of loving him far beyond their own natural capacity" (CCC 52).
- Even though we had turned away from the Lord, even though we had broken our bond with the Lord, he continues to call us back.
- We have the fullness of revelation in Jesus Christ, but the world does not. So we have to pray and go out and proclaim the Gospel.

Take It to **Prayer**

Father in heaven, we thank you. We thank you for revealing yourself to us. We thank you for giving yourself to us because there is so much about you that we can never possibly know or imagine if you had not revealed yourself to us. Lord, you reveal yourself obviously in your creatures, in this creation. But in a particular way, you have reached out to us and revealed your heart to us. You have revealed your identity to us. Keep revealing your heart to us. Keep revealing your identity to us, so that we can know you, so that we can love you as you are, since we know that you love us as we are. In Jesus' name, we pray. Amen.

Dive **Deeper**

Praise God for revealing himself to his creation! Consider God's plan for you today. How can you welcome his love and receive him well?

Reflect on the **Faith**

- Jesus did not establish a new religion. He fulfilled the Old Covenant and established the new and everlasting covenant.
- All the stories of the Old Testament, such as the stories of Abraham and the patriarchs and the prophets, point to where we are living right now.
- "The patriarchs, prophets, and certain other Old Testament figures have been and always will be honored as saints" (CCC 61).
- The letter to the Hebrews talks about these people, who have gone before us. They are the great "cloud of witnesses" that surround us (Hebrews 12:1).
- These stages of revelation happened in real life, in real time, to real people. Generations upon generations got to know God slowly, as nations were formed, wars were fought, and lives were lived. God was moving slowly, for our sake.
- If God revealed himself all at once in a massively overwhelming way, we might not be free to say yes or no to him. It would be difficult to reject him. But if we are not free to reject him, we are not free to love him.

Take It to **Prayer**

Father in heaven, you call us into being, and you reveal yourself to us because you want us to know you. You want us to have a relationship with you. This knowledge of you is oriented toward relationship. So one of your messages, one of the things that you remind us of, as you continue to reveal yourself, is you remind us of hope, the hope that regardless of whatever stage we are at right now—and are knowing you and are following you—you remind us to not give up. You remind us that you are not going to give up. You remind us that you reveal the deepest part of your heart to us as we just have to keep walking, like those patriarchs, like Abraham, Isaac, and Jacob, like their wives and like their children, like the prophets, like our Lord Jesus, who continued to walk even when walking was difficult, even when he was weighed down by the Cross that was meant for us but that he carried for us. Lord God, give us the hope to not stop walking, especially when things are darkest. Help us to have the hope to continue to know that when we are walking, you are walking with us. Give us hope to conquer discouragement. Give us hope to conquer despair. We make this prayer in the mighty name of Jesus, our Lord. Amen.

Dive **Deeper**

OUR FATHER IN FAITH

The Bible speaks of Abraham as our father in faith. Here we see him willing to sacrifice his own son in obedience to God. He trusted fully in God and his promised blessings. (See CCC 59.)

Reflect on the **Faith**

- "God has revealed himself fully" in his Son, Jesus Christ (CCC 73).
- Sometimes, we want God to give us a different answer. So we look all over the place for different revelations. But the Church says very clearly that there will be no further revelation. Why? Because Jesus is the fullness of revelation.
- Revelation is "complete," but it is not "completely explicit" yet. This is one of the reasons why the Church has ecumenical councils.
- The first council of the Church was in Jerusalem in the first years of Christianity, to determine whether Christians had to be circumcised to be baptized.
- There is such a thing as a private revelation. Even if the Church approves a private revelation, there is nothing that requires a Catholic to believe in it.
- Ecclesiastical approval of a private revelation means that its message contains nothing contrary to faith and morality. A private revelation can introduce new emphases or give rise to new forms of piety or deepen older ones. But, as we have seen, we are not required to believe in a specific private revelation.

Take It to **Prayer**

Father in heaven, thank you. Thank you for bringing us to this day. Thank you for bringing us just past a week of listening to the Catechism, *bringing us into day 9 today. We are so grateful, not just for the gift of all that you have done with the Jewish people, all that you have done in establishing covenants with them, but also in fulfilling the covenant and establishing the new and eternal covenant in Jesus Christ, who is the "mediator and fullness of all revelation." Help us to receive him, to receive you, your revelation in Christ and through this Church. We make this prayer in the mighty name of Jesus Christ, our Lord. Amen.*

Dive **Deeper**

How can we tell the difference between official Church teaching and theological opinion?

The *Catechism* asks us to cultivate an attitude of "docility in charity" toward those who teach with "the legitimate authority of the Church," so that we listen with a predisposition to be taught (CCC 2037). But this does not mean that we should accept everything that individual priests or theologians—or even the pope—say or write as equally authoritative. Sometimes they are just offering us their own best theological view on a matter. They should certainly help their hearers and readers to know when they are presenting official Church teaching (using words such as, "The Church teaches that ...") and when they are offering just their own opinion ("My view would be ..." or "I think that ..."). And, of course, it is crucial that they present official Church teaching accurately.

Unfortunately, this kind of clarity is not always present. And the Church wants us to have the confidence that we can discern the difference between authentic Church teaching and mere theological opinion. This is one reason why the *Catechism* is so important. St. John Paul II tells us in his introductory letter *Laetamur Magnopere* that the *Catechism* was given to us precisely to be "a 'sure and authentic reference text'" for teaching Catholic doctrine. This is one of its great points of value for all of us, that we can always go to the *Catechism* to find God's saving doctrine and therefore be able to measure what we read and hear against the truth contained in its pages.

Further reading: John Paul II, apostolic letter *Fidei Depositum*

Reflect on the **Faith**

- Today we are reading about how God has transmitted to us divine revelation through the apostles, and it has come down to us today.
- We will talk about how Scripture and Tradition go hand in hand.
- "Tradition" refers to the "handing on" of divine revelation.
- Revelation comes to us from God's love. St. Paul's letter to Timothy says, "God 'desires all men to be saved and to come to the knowledge of the truth'" (1 Timothy 2:4; see CCC 74).
- Revelation was given to us through the apostles' preaching. We would not have the Bible if it were not for Tradition. We need both Scripture and Tradition.
- St. Paul wrote to Timothy, "What you have heard from me before many witnesses entrust to faithful men who will be able to teach others also" (2 Timothy 2:2). Here St. Paul, who entrusted the teaching to Timothy, tells him to do that as well. This verse reveals three generations of that handing on.
- The early Church Fathers talked about apostolic succession. Pope Clement, writing around the year 80, highlighted apostolic succession in his letter to the Corinthians, showing this is the way God's revelation has been handed on to us. (See Clement, *Letter to the Corinthians*, 42, 44).
- When Judas died, the apostles replaced him with Matthias (see Acts 1:26). With the death of each apostle, a successor bishop is called, ordained, and entrusted with the same apostolic authority.
- God wants to give to us the full truth. Jesus Christ has revealed the full truth to his Church, and the Church has taught this truth to us.

Take It to **Prayer**

Father in heaven, we give you thanks and praise as we begin this day. We just ask you to please be with us. Open our minds and open our hearts so that we can receive what you want to hand on to us—what has been handed down from the very beginning: that you, Lord Jesus, that you had revealed yourself in your fullness to the apostles, and they have handed that on to us. You gave them your Holy Spirit to enlighten and enliven their faith, and they have handed that on to us. Help us to receive that today. Help us to receive what has been handed on so that we cannot just know about this, not just know about you, but that we can live it and we can love you. We make this prayer in Jesus' name. Amen.

Dive **Deeper**

JESUS CALLS PETER AND ANDREW

Here we see Jesus calling Peter and Andrew. They are to become "fishers of men" (Matthew 4:19). It is on the foundation of the apostles, specially chosen and sent (the word apostle literally means "one who is sent") by Christ, that the Church's faith is built. (See CCC 75.)

Reflect on the **Faith**

- The teaching office of the Church is called the Magisterium—the bishops of the world united with the pope.
- St. Paul's first letter to the Corinthians might be one of the earliest documents we have from the Church that is contained in the New Testament—and this letter was not written until around AD 50. The entire New Testament was not written and compiled until much later. So Sacred Tradition precedes Sacred Scripture.
- This does not mean that those people without the New Testament Scriptures were not Christians or members of the Church. It means that they had another source of divine revelation.
- The Protestant Reformation is built on "Scripture alone," which is the idea that all we need for faith is the Bible. However, if Scripture is the sole rule of faith, the Bible would teach this. It does not.
- There is a difference between what we call "big T" (or Sacred) Tradition and "small t" tradition. Sacred Tradition "comes from the apostles and hands on what they received from Jesus' teaching and example and what they learned from the Holy Spirit" (CCC 83). Sacred Tradition does not change. It is established. It is expressed in the Church's dogmas and doctrines.
- "Small t" tradition includes "various theological, disciplinary, liturgical, or devotional" practices of the Church (CCC 83). These can change. One example is the tradition of abstaining from meat on Fridays.

Take It to **Prayer**

Father in heaven, you have made us for yourself, and our hearts are restless until they rest in you. Inflame that desire that we have to know you. Inflame the desire that we have to be found by you. And inflame that desire that we have to find you. You reveal your heart to us. Help us to reveal our hearts to you. Help us not to be numb to the reality that you are. And help us not to be numb to the reality that you are love. We make this prayer in the mighty name of Jesus Christ, our Lord. Amen.

Dive **Deeper**

Can you explain the difference between "big T" Tradition and "little t" tradition?

The word "tradition" literally means "that which is handed on." Sacred Tradition—that is, "big T" Tradition—is one of the sources of divine revelation that is handed on by the apostles, who in turn received their teaching and way of worshipping, praying, and living from Jesus himself. The Lord taught them how to pray, how to celebrate the Eucharist, how to live the Beatitudes, and so on, and the apostles faithfully handed this on. We see Sacred Tradition being handed on in the first moments after Pentecost when the apostles initiated the new converts into the Christian faith and life (see Acts 2:42). In the Prologue, the *Catechism* reminds us of how this Sacred Tradition underpins everything that is to follow in the rest of the *Catechism* (see CCC 3). "Big T" Tradition hands on the essential and fundamental elements of faith and life and applies universally and in all ages.

In every age, Sacred Tradition is handed on through many "little t" traditions. Thus, for instance, the Incarnate Lord in the fullness of his divinity and humanity is adored and reverenced through particular devotions ("little t" traditions) such as devotion to the Sacred Heart of Jesus. Tradition also gives us different rites to celebrate the sacrament of the Holy Eucharist, and the Church prepares people in different ways to participate in these rites (see CCC 1200). "Little t" traditions can be very local and specific in character—for example, how children in a particular time and place dress to receive their First Holy Communion.

Key reading: CCC 3, 80–87, 478, 1200, 2669

Reflect on the **Faith**

- A dogma is a truth revealed by God that the Magisterium of the Church has declared to be binding.
- "If our life is upright, our intellect and heart will be open to welcome the light shed by the dogmas of faith" (CCC 89).
- Some people say that dogmas are too confining, but dogmas provide boundaries that encourage us to go deeper in our faith without the danger of straying from it.
- Dogmas are not just boundaries, though. They are "lights along the path of faith" (CCC 89). They are gifts from God. We must receive them as gifts.
- When we hear the teachings of the Church—Sacred Scripture and Sacred Tradition and the Magisterium of the Church—we accept them and come to understand them and live them out (see CCC 93).
- The whole point of this is that we can know God accurately, we can know ourselves accurately, and we can know his will more fully so that we can do it.

Take It to **Prayer**

Father in heaven, we thank you. We thank you for this day. We thank you for bringing us to day 12—bringing us to the end of this second week of listening and learning about how you have spoken to us, how much you love us, that in a plan of sheer goodness you sent your only begotten Son. You have given us your Holy Spirit. You have given us a Church. And you have given us your Word, both in flesh and in Scripture. And you have made us members of your Body. So Lord God, we ask you to please help us to be faithful. Help us to be faithful to what you have called us to. Help us to receive the dogmas that you have made explicit. Help us to live out the truth. Let us not just be hearers of the Word but doers of the Word as well. We make this prayer in the mighty name of Jesus Christ, our Lord. Amen.

Dive **Deeper**

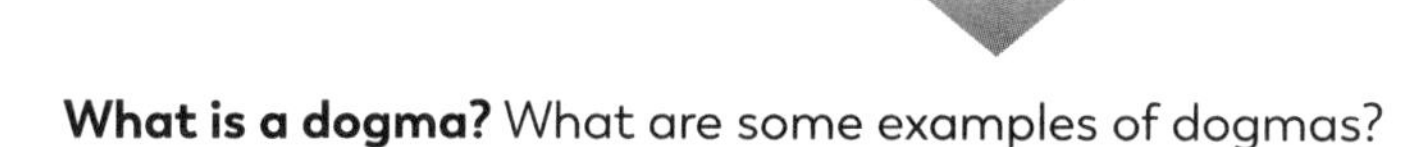

What is a dogma? What are some examples of dogmas?

As the *Catechism* states, dogmas are "lights along the path of faith" that "illuminate it and make it secure" (CCC 89). This is a powerful image. The purpose of every dogma is to provide the necessary light for us to see where we are going on the path toward heaven, to keep us from losing our way or falling. The *Catechism* describes a dogma as the expression of the fullest teaching authority of the Church when she defines a truth that is either an aspect of God's revelation or necessarily connected to revelation.

Some examples of dogmas: the Trinitarian nature of God—i.e., that the Son is "consubstantial" with the Father—defined at the Council of Nicaea in AD 325; the hypostatic union—i.e., that Jesus Christ has two natures, human and divine, in one divine Person—defined at the Councils of Ephesus in 431 and Chalcedon in 451; and the Immaculate Conception of the Blessed Virgin Mary, proclaimed by Pope Pius IX in 1854.

Of course, all teachings, or "doctrines," of the Magisterium of the Church light our path, but dogmas are especially bright lights that keep us from stumbling along the journey of faith. They are the foundations upon which our Faith is built, upon which every teaching of the Church is rooted.

Key reading: CCC 88–95, 495

Reflect on the **Faith**

- As St. Paul writes to the Thessalonians, "So then, brethren, stand firm and hold to the traditions which you were taught by us, either by word of mouth or by letter" (2 Thessalonians 2:15). This is one place where it is made clear that Sacred Tradition and Sacred Scripture are equally important.
- We recognize the role of the Church to be able to give us divine revelation.
- The canon of Scripture, the list of the seventy-three books of the Bible, comes from Sacred Tradition. Everyone who reads the Bible and accepts this canon is relying upon an authority outside of the Bible. They are relying upon Sacred Tradition.
- Who the Church is and what the Church believes is revealed in the way it prays and lives.
- The phrase *lex orandi, lex credendi*—"the law of prayer is the law of belief"—means that the way the Church prays reveals what it believes.
- In 1 Timothy 3:14–15, St. Paul says, "I hope to come to you soon, but I am writing these instructions to you so that, if I am delayed, you may know how one ought to behave in the household of God, which is the Church of the living God, the pillar and bulwark of the truth." So the Church is the "pillar" and "bulwark" of the truth.

Take It to **Prayer**

Father in heaven, Lord God, we thank you so much. We thank you for continuing to reach out to us. We thank you for continuing to speak to us. We thank you for continuing to call us closer to you. Lord God, you have not abandoned this age. You have not abandoned this generation. But you, in the power of your Holy Spirit, continue to pour out your goodness, your grace, your love, and your truth upon every heart that seeks you. Lord God, you even pour out your grace and truth and love upon hearts that don't seek you. God, help us. Help us to be hearts that are open to your love, that are open to your grace, that are open to your truth, and help us to never forget what you've done in our lives. Seal the knowledge of you and seal the knowledge of truth in our hearts. Seal the graces that you have given to us deeply into our lives and help us always, always to pursue you because you will never stop at pursuing us. In Jesus' name, we pray. Amen.

Dive **Deeper**

How can we trust the Magisterium when popes have been sinful and made mistakes in the past?

The Catholic Church was founded by Christ, who endowed his apostles with the authority to teach in his name. The Church, then, is the defender of the Gospel of Christ, and is his infallible witness in the world. That said, the Church is made up of sinful human beings, with popes and bishops in its history who lived sinful lives. Even today, the Church's leaders are not perfect, so how can we trust what they say? Quite simply, we can trust the Magisterium because Jesus assures us that we can.

Even St. Peter, the apostle Jesus chose as the first pope, denied knowing him three times. Yet Jesus made Peter the "rock" upon which he would build his Church (see Matthew 16:18). While leaders of the Church may be sinful, we can trust what they teach within the Magisterium because of the authority Jesus has given them. Through the charism of their office and the protection of the Holy Spirit, every pope preserves the essentials of the Faith. This is Christ's gift to his Church. So the sinfulness of its members, even its leaders, cannot change its constant teaching on matters of the Faith or morality. We should trust in the Holy Spirit's protection of the Church, and we should pray for our priests, bishops, and the pope, that they might be holy and faithful to their calling.

Further reading: Galatians 2:11

Reflect on the **Faith**

- God could have revealed himself in any way he wanted. But he spoke to us "in human words" (CCC 101).
- God stoops down to us and speaks to us as a father speaks to his children. This is God's self-revelation.
- Even if we do not understand everything in the Scriptures, even if it does not really pertain to our lives that day, we are fed.
- You and I cooperate freely with God, but in this freedom, God gives us his grace to do what we could never do without his grace. This is what happened when God employed the use of the human authors of Sacred Scripture. This is one of the reasons why Matthew's Gospel sounds different from Luke's Gospel.
- "Scripture firmly, faithfully, and without error teach[es] that truth which God, for the sake of our salvation, wishes to see confided to the Sacred Scriptures" (CCC 107).
- When we pick up the Scriptures, we are encountering God, who is alive.

Take It to **Prayer**

Father in heaven, we thank you so much. Thank you for loving us to a point where you want to reveal yourself to us. Thank you for loving us in such a way that you have given us your Word, your only beloved Son, your only begotten Son, Jesus Christ, your Word made flesh. And how Jesus Christ has revealed you, fully, to humanity. And how your Holy Spirit has continued to operate. How the Holy Spirit has continued to move in the people of God. How the Holy Spirit has continued to guide us. We ask you to, please, send that same Holy Spirit to renew in our hearts a love of your Word, to renew our hearts and understanding and desire for your Word, and to enlighten our minds so that we can understand you and understand your Word, all so that we can follow you more closely. In Jesus' name, we pray. Amen.

Dive **Deeper**

In prayer, ask God to nourish you with the living Word. Ask him to lead you to a deeper understanding of the truth confided in the Sacred Scriptures so that you may grow in your relationship with him.

Reflect on the **Faith**

- Today, we are going to talk about how the Holy Spirit is not only the inspirer of Sacred Scripture but the one who shows us what it means.
- How do we as Catholics interpret the Bible? This is an important question to answer. In paragraphs 109 to 114, The *Catechism* gives us some basic principles.
- First, we look at the whole Bible. We should never take a text of Scripture out of context. We always have to read every passage in light of the whole Bible.
- Secondly, we "*read the Scripture within 'the living Tradition of the whole Church'* " (CCC 113). So we do not read Scripture on its own but also look, for example, to the Fathers of the Church and Sacred Tradition.
- Thirdly, we have to "*be attentive to the analogy of faith*" (CCC 114). The word "analogy" refers to a proportion, so this highlights the fact that every truth of the Faith is in relationship to every other truth of the Faith. We cannot allow a new interpretation that is contradictory, out of line, or disproportionate to the other truths of the Faith.
- When we read Scripture, we always keep in mind all that God has revealed in Scripture, in Tradition, and through the Magisterium.

Take It to **Prayer**

Heavenly Father, we thank you so much. We are so grateful. We are so grateful for you. That you are, and that you reveal yourself to us, that you reveal the depth of your heart to us. That you gave us your only beloved Son so that we might not perish but that we could have eternal life. And you give us your Holy Spirit to guide us and to continue to guide us into all truth. Lord, help us to read the Scriptures according to your Spirit. Help us to live according to your Spirit so that we can pray according to your Spirit and that we may, by your will and by your gracious gift, dwell with you, Father, Son, and Holy Spirit, for all eternity. We make this prayer in Jesus' name. Amen.

Dive **Deeper**

ST. JEROME AT WORK

This picture shows St. Jerome and his brothers in the scriptorium, a room where manuscripts were meticulously copied. The Church owes much to St. Jerome for his translation and interpretation of the Bible.

Reflect on the **Faith**

- There are two main "senses" of Scripture: (1) the literal sense, and (2) the spiritual sense (see CCC 115–117). Whenever we read the Bible, we read it according to these two senses.

- The literal sense is the more obvious sense. It is what the text says on a literal level.

- The spiritual sense is broken into three: the "allegorical" sense, the "moral" sense, and the "anagogical" sense. The allegorical sense is how this applies to Jesus; the moral sense is how it applies to our lives; and the anagogical sense is how it applies to the end of time.

- As St. Thomas Aquinas said, "All other senses of Sacred Scripture are based on the literal" (quoted in CCC 116).

- The example that the *Catechism* uses to explain these senses is the story of the Israelites crossing the Red Sea. The literal sense of this passage is that the people of Israel actually walked through the parted waters of the Red Sea.

- In the allegorical sense, the crossing of the Red Sea points to how Jesus died, descended to hell, and rose again from the dead. The crossing of the Red Sea also points to how Christians enter into the waters of Baptism and come out the other side with freedom and with life.

- As St. Augustine said, "I would not believe in the Gospel, had not the authority of the Catholic Church already moved me" (quoted in CCC 119). He was living close enough to the original events of Christ's life, death, and resurrection that he knew that the Church predated the New Testament. Again, the authority of the Church comes before the authority of the Bible in time.

Take It to **Prayer**

Father in heaven, we give you thanks. We give you praise because we know this. We know that you are the author of Sacred Scripture. We know that you used human beings with all of their gifts, with all their wisdom, with all their flaws, with all their lack of knowledge, with all their style and preference, and just their personality. Lord God, you used them to convey your Word to the world. And you still do that in different ways, right? You still use us. You still use us, with all of our wisdom, and all of our failures, with all of our weaknesses, and with all of our foolishness, with all our strengths, and gifts, and personalities. Lord God, you continue to use and work with us, to bring your Word to the world. When we embody your Word, Lord God, when we live out your truth, you are working in this world. And we ask you to please help us not only hear these words but be shaped by them so that we can live by them. Help us to live by your Word. In Jesus' name, we pray. Amen.

Dive **Deeper**

Do Scripture, the Magisterium, and Tradition oppose each other? Take ten minutes to watch the Ascension Presents video "Where Is That in the Bible? Why Catholics Use Scripture and Tradition" to hear Fr. Mike defend these important pillars that support and inform each other in the Catholic Faith, making God all the more present to us in our lives today.

Reflect on the **Faith**

- The *Catechism* lays out the "canon" of Scripture—that is, those books that we acknowledge to have been divinely inspired. These are the books found in a Catholic Bible.
- Sacred Tradition is essential to our acceptance and understanding of Scripture. The apostles handed on Jesus' teachings, guided by the Holy Spirit.
- It is through the living Tradition of the Church that we even know which books are inspired and included in the New Testament.
- It was not until the late fourth century that the books of the New Testament were officially codified, though the texts had been used in the Church for centuries.
- Martin Luther and the Protestant Reformation challenged this canon, so the Council of Trent reaffirmed it in 1546.
- One of the reasons the Church holds councils is to address new questions about the Faith as they arise.

Take It to **Prayer**

Father in heaven, we thank you. We give you praise. You enter into time with us. You enter into this space that we occupy. And you enter into our lives in a very real, in a very true way. Lord God, our lives are messy. And even the way in which we have discovered who you are, you have revealed yourself to us, has been messy. But we trust in you. We trust that you are in the mess. You are in the mess of our lives. You are in the mess of history. You are in the mess of our culture. Because that is where you want to be, where we are, and that is where we live. And so we ask that you please, into the mess, bring clarity; into the brokenness bring healing; into our confusion, bring illumination and bring light, so that we can understand who you are more clearly, who we are more clearly, and that we can love you with all of our hearts. In Jesus' name, we pray, Amen.

Dive **Deeper**

ANCIENT COPY OF BIBLICAL TEXT

The Church, guided by the Holy Spirit, determined the biblical "canon," which is the official list of inspired books. Here we see an ancient copy of Biblical text.

Reflect on the **Faith**

- The Old Testament retains its intrinsic value. All of Scripture has a unity.
- In the Scripture we see typology. In the Old Testament, God reveals things that get fulfilled in the New Testament.
- An example of typology is the Ark of the Covenant. Inside the Ark was the manna from the desert, the Ten Commandments, and Aaron's staff. Those three things symbolize the bread come down from heaven, the Word of God, and the priesthood.
- "The Church 'forcefully and specifically exhorts all the Christian faithful ... to learn "the surpassing knowledge of Jesus Christ," by frequent reading of the divine Scriptures'" (CCC 133).
- As St. Jerome said, "Ignorance of the Scriptures is ignorance of Christ'" (CCC 133).
- The Church, at various times throughout history, emphasized the importance of having a correct translation of the Bible. If someone tells you that the Church once said, "Don't read the Bible," that is incorrect. But the Church may have said, "Don't read *that* Bible."
- Similarly, Bibles were locked up in churches not to prevent access to the Scriptures but to prevent theft of the copies of the Bible, which were very expensive and had to be produced by hand before the invention of the printing press.

Take It to **Prayer**

Father in heaven, we give you praise. And we thank you on this day. We thank you for revealing yourself to us. We thank you for all the years, the countless generations that it took for you to reveal yourself in time to us. We thank you for the fullness of time when you revealed yourself to us in the person of your son, Jesus Christ, Our Lord. Thank you for the Holy Spirit that you sent upon the Church, who continues to lead us, who continues to guide us, who continues to teach us. Give us a love not only just to know more about you, give us a love for Scripture. Put in our hearts a desire to seek after you, a desire to read your Word, a desire to hear your Word proclaimed, and a desire to share your Word with everyone in our lives, with everyone we love, and everyone on this planet, especially for those who have never heard your Word, Lord. Or those who have, they thought they heard your Word, they think they hear your Word, but they are mistaken. We ask that you please correct our mistakes, correct our errors, and bring all of us into the light of your truth. In Jesus' name, we pray. Amen.

Dive **Deeper**

CHRIST FULFILLS THE OLD TESTAMENT

This fourteenth-century painting, The Nativity with the Prophets Isaiah and Ezekiel *depicts the birth of Christ with these two holy men who prophesied the coming of Jesus and the New Covenant. As Christians, we read the Old Testament in light of Christ and his salvific work (CCC 129).*

Reflect on the **Faith**

- There are human authors, but there is also a divine author of Scripture. That is not a contradiction; it is a mystery.
- Everything in God's revelation is about revealing who God is, his very heart.
- We know that the Bible is inerrant—that it is true.
- We remember that we look at the Scriptures according to the literal sense and the spiritual sense. The spiritual always rests on the literal.
- *Exegesis* is taking out of Scripture what it is trying to tell us and applying it to our lives. This is what we are supposed to do with Scripture.
- There are 46 books in the Old Testament and 27 books in the New Testament.
- As Psalm 119:105 says, "Your word is a lamp to my feet and a light to my path" (see CCC 141).

Take It to **Prayer**

Father in heaven, we thank you. Thank you for bringing us through another chapter. Thank you for bringing us through this revelation of you, the revelation of who you are, the revelation of your heart, and revelation of how you have come to us in time, in reality, in history. Lord God, we know that our times are not easy to live in, but there are no easy times in which to live. We know that our own personal histories are not clean and not perfect, but there are no histories that are clean and perfect. And so, just as you have entered into time, just as you have entered into history, we ask you to enter into this moment in our time. We ask you to enter into this part of our story in our own history and do what you will and help us to do your will. In Jesus' name, we pray. Amen.

Dive **Deeper**

Is the *Catechism* inerrant, like the Bible?

The Church reserves the term "inerrant" for the Sacred Scriptures which, having God as their primary author, "firmly, faithfully, and without error teach that truth which God, for the sake of our salvation, wished to see confided" in them (*Dei Verbum* 11; quoted in CCC 107). The Church does not claim that the authors of the *Catechism* were "inspired" in the same way that the human authors of the Bible were. Still, St. John Paul II called the *Catechism* a "sure norm" for teaching the faith since its contents are "attested to or illumined" by the Scriptures and Tradition, as interpreted by the Magisterium. The mission of the *Catechism* is to "guard" and provide a summary of the deposit of the faith, enabling the faithful transmission of divine revelation as contained in Scripture and Tradition.

In addition, the *Catechism* shows us how the Scriptures have been interpreted within the Tradition of the Church. It thus helps us know how we may understand the text of the Bible, providing a secure path for us into a faithful reading of Scripture. The *Catechism* and the Bible should therefore be read together.

Key reading: St. John Paul II, apostolic constitution *Fidei Depositum*, CCC 105–108, 134–141

Reflect on the **Faith**

- Paragraph 142 sums up what we have been reading in the last few days: "*By his Revelation*, 'the invisible God, from the fullness of his love, addresses men as his friends, and moves among them'" (CCC 142). Jesus fulfills this in his words and deeds.

- Then the *Catechism* highlights, "The adequate response to this invitation is faith" (CCC 142).

- There is a difference between believing *in* God and *believing* God. We can believe that God exists. We can believe that God has revealed himself. We can believe all the articles of faith. But *believing* God means something more. It implies some kind of relationship, some kind of action.

- To paraphrase the letter of James, we believe that God is one. That is good. But even the demons believe that. (See James 2:19.) Often, Jesus performed exorcisms, and the demons said that they knew who Jesus was (see Luke 4:41). The demons knew the truth, but that is not good enough.

- To have a feeling of trust is wonderful. But it is limited.

- Faith means submitting our will to God. It means saying, "God, you have my whole being. What I know, what I think, what I choose, my intellect and my will, I'm submitting to you and to your will." This is so important.

- Jesus tells us that not everyone who says "Lord, Lord" will enter the kingdom of heaven but only the ones who do the will of the Father (see Matthew 7:21).

- Mary is an example for us. The angel Gabriel did not give Mary the whole plan. He gave only the next step. Walking in faith means not having the whole vision of what the future will bring.

Take It to **Prayer**

Father in heaven, we know that you have revealed yourself to us. And we know that you are calling us into a relationship with you. We know that you are calling us to respond to your revelation. As you have revealed your heart, you are calling us to respond by trusting you. You are calling us to respond by doing your will. You are calling us to respond by placing our faith in you and everything you have done and everything you have promised. And we do that by conforming our will to yours. We can only do that by the power of your Holy Spirit. None of us can do that on our own, on our own strength, on our own goodness, on our own merits. We don't have any to offer. But only by your Spirit, only by the power of your grace and your goodness. So please, Lord God, send us your grace. Send us your Holy Spirit so that we can respond as you are calling us to. In Jesus' name, we pray. Amen.

Dive **Deeper**

What fears are preventing you from stepping into faith and trusting in God completely? Pray for the power of the Holy Spirit to strengthen your obedience of faith today as you boldly pursue your relationship with God in steadfast trust.

Reflect on the **Faith**

- Faith is both a grace and a human act. It is a gift that comes from God, but it is also a completely free act on our part, where we freely accept and cooperate.
- Faith is not just having a feeling.
- No one can come to a deep place of allegiance to God without God's help.
- God wants all people to be saved.
- Obeying God does not strip us of our freedom; rather, it is an exercise of our freedom. Freedom is not the ability to do whatever we want. It is the power to do what we ought. If God exists and is good, then I ought to have faith in him and choose to follow him.
- As the saying goes, if we believe what we like in the Gospel and reject what we don't, it is not the Gospel we believe in but ourselves.
- It is right and just to entrust ourselves wholly to God and believe absolutely what he says because he is God; he is Truth itself.

Take It to **Prayer**

Father in heaven, we give you thanks and praise. May your name be known around this entire world. May your name be known. May your identity be known by every person who breathes on this planet. We ask that you please make yourself known to us. Help us to have faith in you. Help us to freely assent to you. Give us this personal adherence to you, as we know that you're not a thing, God. You are a who. You are the Father, Son, and Holy Spirit. And we can trust ourselves to you now. We ask that you please help us to entrust ourselves and adhere ourselves to you for all time, into eternity, by your grace. In Jesus' name, we pray. Amen.

Dive **Deeper**

Recall a time when your belief in God was challenged. Were you experiencing pain, fear, loneliness, or desolation? Entrust yourself to him today with a renewed faith in his love for you and a desire to remain in communion with him forever.

Reflect on the **Faith**

- That we grow in understanding of our faith, that we know the one in whom we trust, that we trust freely, and that we hold on through our whole lives are all critically important.
- When we grow in faith, sometimes our faith is helped by signs and proofs. Ultimately, though, we are not simply believing *in* God, we are believing *God*. We are believing in him because we know that he is true.
- What moves us to believe is the authority of God himself. At the same time, faith does not go contrary to our reason. God does not ask us to "turn off" our reason to have faith.
- Miracles, prophecies, and the growth and holiness of the Church are credible motives for belief.
- Faith is certain because we are trusting in God, who cannot lie.
- There is no dichotomy between faith and science. Truths do not contradict each other. (See CCC 159.)
- As St. John Paul II once said, "The Church proposes; she imposes nothing."[2] Faith can never be coerced.
- Scripture has made it very clear that "without faith it is impossible to please" God (Hebrews 11:6; see CCC 161).
- St. Paul wrote to Timothy, "By rejecting conscience, certain persons have made shipwreck of their faith" (1 Timothy 1:19; see CCC 162). We know that we have to pray for the gift of final perseverance because without God's help, we will not make it to the end.

Take It to **Prayer**

Father in heaven, we know that on sunny days and days where everything is going well, that you are God. We also know that when we are in the valley of the shadow of death, you are still God. We know that when we have everything we have ever wanted, you are trustworthy. And when we are so confused and feel so lost and so alone, you are still trustworthy. Help us to trust in you. Help us to continue to adhere to you. Help us to continue to submit our intellect and will to you. Help us to belong to you fully. Not only in this moment, but in every single moment of our lives, so that at the end of our lives, we can have that grace of final perseverance, clinging to you even in darkness. Help us to always know that what was true in the light is also true in the darkness. Be with us in both, Lord God. In Jesus' name, we pray. Amen.

Dive **Deeper**

JACOB WRESTLES WITH GOD

In the person of Jacob, pictured here wrestling with the angel of the Lord, we can see ourselves and our own honest struggles with the faith (see CCC 157). Despite his own "wrestling," Jacob never lost faith in God and his promises.

Reflect on the **Faith**

- We have faith, yet we continue to walk in a world that is broken (see CCC 164).
- "Faith is a personal act" yet "not an isolated act. No one can believe alone" (CCC 166).
- "Salvation comes from God alone; but because we receive the life of faith through the Church, she is our mother" (CCC 169).
- We have what we long for in faith. We possess our Lord, and he possesses us.
- C. S. Lewis wrote, "Heaven, once attained, will work backwards and turn even ... agony into a glory ... [but] the bad man's past already conforms to his badness and is filled only with dreariness. And that is why ... the Blessed will say 'We have never lived anywhere except in Heaven,' and the Lost, 'We were always in Hell.'"[3] If we keep saying yes to the Lord, then in a sense we are living in heaven now.
- We have not given ourselves faith just as we have not given ourselves life (see CCC 166). Faith has been handed to us by the Church.

Take It to **Prayer**

Father in heaven, we give you praise. We give you glory. We believe in you. As individuals, we can say, "I believe in you, Father." We can say, "I trust you, Jesus." We can say, "I need you, Holy Spirit." And that is all true. Today, we also say we believe, we need, and we trust you because we are not alone. In fact, Father, this community of people who are listening to this Catechism and striving to learn more and more about you, striving to have faith that seeks understanding—we need your help. We need each other's prayers. And we cannot do this without you. Jesus, we know that without you, we can do nothing. So come to our need, come to our weakness, come to our aid with your help. I make this prayer in your name, Jesus Christ. Amen.

Dive **Deeper**

Think of someone in your life who may be feeling isolated or alone. Pray that this person will encounter God's love in a profound way and experience a new desire to grow in faith and understanding.

Reflect on the **Faith**

- The Church's role is to faithfully guard the Faith. St. Paul, writing to Timothy, called the Church "the pillar and bulwark of the truth" (1 Timothy 3:15; see CCC 171).
- St. Irenaeus of Lyons was one of the Early Church Fathers with a direct connection to St. John the Apostle. St. Irenaeus said, "The Church, though scattered throughout the whole world, even to the ends of the earth, having received the faith from the apostles and their disciples ... guards [this preaching and faith] with care, as dwelling in but a single house" (quoted in CCC 173).
- One of the marks of the Church is that it is one.
- St. Irenaeus says, "For though languages differ throughout the world, the content of the Tradition is one and the same." What the Church teaches "is true and solid, in which one and the same way of salvation appears throughout the whole world" (quoted in CCC 174).
- From the very beginning, the Church has stood for unity. In the Councils, the Church had to come together, invoke the Holy Spirit, and address big questions. The answers that they recognized have been passed on throughout the whole world so that we have one united Faith—one Church.
- Our prayer today is, "Lord, I don't have all the answers. Your Church is going to guide me into all truth by the power of your Holy Spirit. Help me today not just so I can know more about you but so that, in knowing you, I can love you better and follow you better."

Take It to **Prayer**

Father in heaven, we give you praise and glory. We thank you so much for bringing us to this moment. We thank you for the fact that you have passed on your Word. You passed on your revelation of yourself to us, through the Church. Lord God, we also know that we do not simply believe in formulas. We believe in the realities that those formulas express. We know we don't believe in the idea of you as Father, and as Son, and as Holy Spirit. We believe in the reality: you are Father, you are Son, you are Holy Spirit. We don't believe merely in the idea that you came to save us from our sins, but in the reality that you have done this, and you continue to do this by sending out your Holy Spirit and meeting us ever new with your mercy every morning. So, Lord, help us to continue to recognize that you are not merely an idea. You are Reality itself. You are Being itself. Help us to be aware of your reality. Help us to be aware of your being. Help us to be aware of you this day and every day. In Jesus' name, we pray. Amen.

Dive **Deeper**

The Church says that the Catholic Faith has remained essentially unchanged since the time of Jesus. But haven't new teachings been proclaimed over the centuries?

Jesus *is* Truth itself (see John 14:6). Through the apostles, he has handed on to us the fullness of truth and life. There is, therefore, "one faith, received from the one Lord, transmitted by one Baptism" (CCC 172). So our Faith is the same Faith taught by Jesus and proclaimed by the apostles.

When we are given something wonderful, it takes time to realize just what we have been given. After telling his disciples that he is the Truth, Jesus promised to send the Spirit to "guide [them] into all the truth" (John 16:13). The fullness of God's revelation was given, and it was for the apostles and then their successors (the bishops) to deepen their understanding of this truth. Thus, the saving truth of the Faith does not change, but it must be *understood* and *manifested* in all ages and cultures. A development in understanding of a particular teaching (see CCC 94) does not involve an overturning or rejection of what went before. It involves making *explicit* something that is *implicit*, unpacking the gift we have been given. In all cases, the Magisterium judges whether a particular development of understanding or expression within a culture (see CCC 854) is faithful to the one unchanging Faith.

Key reading: CCC 94, 170–175

Reflect on the **Faith**

- Our response to God's Revelation is faith. Faith means we do not just say yes intellectually but we give our whole allegiance to God. This is a personal relationship, but at the same time it is communal; we do not come to the Lord in isolation.
- We place our trust in the Lord fully, meaning that we say yes with our whole selves to what he has revealed. That is the challenge of our lives.
- While God's revelation of himself is complete, our understanding of this revelation is going to be limited by our finite minds.
- Deep faith means believing in the one who reveals the truth to us—God himself. We believe in individual teachings of the Faith because we believe in the identity of God, the teacher.
- St. Cyprian says, "No one can have God as Father who does not have the Church as Mother" (quoted in CCC 181). This is because no one comes to faith on their own. Because we trust God, because we have faith in God, we can profess the faith of the Church without hesitation and with great zeal and conviction.
- As we journey in the next couple of days, we are going to keep going deeper and deeper into the Creed. With every step, we are not just trying to learn data. We are trying to say yes to the one who is the author of the data.

Take It to **Prayer**

Father in heaven, we know that you have revealed yourself to us so that we can entrust our entire selves back to you. You revealed the depth of your identity, the depth of your heart, the depth of the relationship that you want with us. We ask that you please give us hearts, give us minds that cannot simply grasp or apprehend the ideas but hearts that trust you. Give us a will that will truly choose to say yes to you when we are certain and when we have questions, when we have no difficulties and when we are faced with difficulties. Lord God, send us your grace. Help us to have the grace of faith, the gift of faith, and then give us the courage to exercise the virtue of faith. We make this prayer in the mighty name of Jesus Christ, Our Lord. Amen.

Dive **Deeper**

How do we submit our intellect and will to God?

We might think that to "submit" means giving up our ability to think and make our own decisions, which is what dictators and tyrants require of their people. But this is not what God is asking of us! "Submitting" our whole selves to God means handing over our intellect (how we think and reason) and our will (how we choose to act) to freely serve and love him, not to become slaves but to become his children.

How do we do this? Serving God completely can be hard because we do not fully understand his will for us, or his way seems too difficult or uncomfortable, or we cannot reconcile our personal weaknesses and sufferings with what he is asking of us. We need to remember, though, that we are not "on our own." The Lord is always present, giving us the grace needed in every moment in every situation. We must pray and ask him for the grace to submit to his loving will, even when we do not fully "get it." This also means frequenting the sacraments of Reconciliation and the Holy Eucharist, because the closer we come to God, the more we can submit to him with trust.

Further reading: Vatican II, *Dei Verbum*, 5–6, *Gaudium et Spes*, 16–17; Paul VI, encyclical letter *Mysterium Fidei*; Luke 9:23, John 14:15, Hebrews 12:1–2.

Reflect on the **Faith**

- The word "creed" comes from the Latin *credo*, "I believe." We use this term because the creeds typically begin this way (see CCC 187).
- "The Greek word *symbolon* meant half of a broken object ... The broken parts were placed together to verify the bearer's identity. The symbol of faith, then, is a sign of recognition and communion between believers" (CCC 188).
- The Apostles' Creed sums up what Christians believed from the beginning. Then the Council of Nicaea, which composed the Nicene Creed, was convened in the year 325 to respond to the question of what it means to say that Jesus is the son of God.
- Modern times have seen the greatest number of martyrs for the Faith, according to some researchers. Throughout the world, Christians continue to be persecuted, tortured, and killed for our Faith. These are people who believe exactly what you and I believe. And because of that, they are now being persecuted.
- The Nicene Creed has three parts, addressing God the Father, the Creator; Jesus Christ, who redeems us; and the Holy Spirit (see CCC 190).

Take It to **Prayer**

Father in heaven, we know that you have revealed yourself to us so that we can entrust our entire selves back to you. You revealed the depth of your identity, the depth of your heart, the depth of the relationship that you want with us. We ask that you please give us hearts, give us minds that cannot simply grasp or apprehend the ideas but hearts that trust you. Give us a will that will truly choose to say yes to you when we are certain and when we have questions, when we have no difficulties and when we are faced with difficulties. Lord God, send us your grace. Help us to have the grace of faith, the gift of faith, and then give us the courage to exercise the virtue of faith. We make this prayer in the mighty name of Jesus Christ, our Lord. Amen.

Dive **Deeper**

In prayer, praise God for revealing himself to you. Ask for the courage to continue pursuing him courageously, even amid difficult situations that may challenge your faith in him.

Reflect on the **Faith**

- To be a Christian is not simply to believe in Jesus; it is to believe particular things about Jesus as well.
- There have been many times throughout history when it was necessary to be able to define what it is that Christians believe. That is not meant to put people on the outside but rather to be accurate and to highlight what it is to be on the inside.
- What do we mean when we say "God"? That is vital to be able to know. The Apostles' Creed makes it very clear: "I believe in God, the Father almighty, Creator of heaven and earth, and in Jesus Christ, his only Son, our Lord."
- The Nicene Creed spelled out that Jesus is "true God from true God." He is fully God.
- The creeds have a role in our lives. St. Ambrose calls the Creed "an ever-present guardian; it is, unquestionably, the treasure of our soul" (CCC 197).
- The creed is meant to be a boundary for us so that we do not say something about God that is not true and we do not deny something about God that is true.
- The creed, as an ever-present guardian, continues to lead us in the path of truth so that we can dive more deeply day by day into the reality of who God truly is.

Take It to **Prayer**

Father in heaven, we thank you so much. We thank you for the gift of your Church. We thank you for the gift of revealing yourself to us. We thank you for the gift of communicating the truth about your heart, the truth about your identity to us in the midst of this confusing and uncertain world. We know that, Lord, you work through history. We know that you are present in history. You are present in world events. We know that you interact with us and you are alive. You are guiding us. And through guiding us, you guide the course of world affairs. Lord God, you are perfect, even when this world is not perfect. You are good, even when we are not good. You are true, even when we struggle and strain to understand what is true. Open our hearts, Lord God. Open our hearts to love your will. Open our minds to understand what it is you wish to teach us this day and every day. In Jesus' name, we pray. Amen.

Dive **Deeper**

THE FORMATION OF THE CREED

We have depicted here the First Council of Nicaea (AD 325). It was at this Council that the Nicene Creed was formulated. (See CCC 195.)

Reflect on the **Faith**

- For the next few days, we're talking about the mystery of God.
- God is "ineffable." He is "unchangeable, incomprehensible, almighty" (CCC 202). Sometimes we can treat those words lightly and think we know all about God, but God is so much more than we can grasp.
- God is the creator of heaven and earth. All space, all time, and everything that exists comes from God.
- God is one Being. There are not three gods. God is one God in three Divine Persons.
- The Trinity is a mystery. God's identity is the deepest mystery that any of us could ever even begin to ponder.
- "God has a name; he is not an anonymous force." He has made it possible for us to know him deeply and speak to him by name. (See CCC 203.)

Take It to **Prayer**

Father in heaven, we give you praise. You are the Father in heaven. You are the Father on earth. You are the Lord of everything. And you have sent us your Son, Jesus Christ, who is also God, to be our Savior. And you have sent us your Holy Spirit, who is also God, to guide us and to sanctify us. So Father, Son, and Holy Spirit, one God, help us to understand your nature, help us to understand what you are, and help us to understand even more fully who you are, that we might be drawn into your heart even more deeply. We make this prayer in the mighty name of Jesus Christ, our Lord, and the power of the Holy Spirit, for the glory of God the Father. Amen.

Dive **Deeper**

Sit in wonder and appreciation for the mystery of the Most Holy Trinity. How does this understanding of God's nature draw you closer to him?

Reflect on the **Faith**

- God's people have cared for the Lord God's name and have not just avoided using it irreverently, but have only wanted to use it in the most sacred of ways (see CCC 209).
- God is existence himself, but he has entered into our lives and put himself into our story.
- If we fully realized the identity of Jesus and our own identity, we would do the same things that Moses did in the divine presence—we would take off our shoes or want to hide our faces. Why? Because here is God, and we are not God.
- When we realize who God is and who we are, we realize our own smallness. We realize his glory. We realize his faithfulness and our faithlessness.
- This is a God who loves us, who draws near to us.
- In John's Gospel, Jesus says, "When you have lifted up the Son of Man, then you will know that I am he" (John 8:28; see CCC 211). Jesus makes it very clear that he is claiming divinity.

Take It to **Prayer**

Father in heaven, you have revealed your heart. You have revealed your name because you want us to be in relationship with you. You want us to share our hearts with you, as you have shared your heart with us. So, this day, we come before you. And we ask that as we call upon your name, you answer quickly, you answer fully, and you help us. Help us to understand who it is you are. Help us to love who you are. And help us to glorify who you are in this life so we can be happy with you forever in the next. In Jesus' name, we pray. Amen.

Dive **Deeper**

MOSES BEFORE THE BURNING BUSH

Here we see Moses before the burning bush. It is before this miraculous bush, aflame but unconsumed, that Moses receives the revelation of God's name (YHWH, "I AM WHO AM") and his mission to save God's people from slavery in Egypt. (See CCC 205.)

Reflect on the **Faith**

- God is existence itself. God is the fullness of being and of every perfection without beginning and without end.
- He has given existence to every created thing. Everything exists in relation to God.
- We are all contingent beings. We are all dependent (or contingent) on something else, on the only necessary being—God.
- God is absolutely faithful. His promises always come true. We can abandon ourselves to the Lord because he is truth. He can neither deceive nor be deceived.
- God has revealed that not only is he truth, but he is love.
- God calls us to worship him because he loves us.
- "By sending his only Son and the Spirit of Love in the fullness of time, God has revealed his innermost secret" (CCC 221).
- God is love; that is his deepest identity. His "innermost secret" is that he is love, and you are made in God's image and likeness (CCC 221).

Take It to **Prayer**

Father in heaven, we know that you are. We affirm that you are. And we declare that you are truth. And we believe that you are love. Lord God, come and meet us, come sustain us, come guide us with your truth. Come lead us more deeply into your heart. Come lead us more deeply into your love. Be with us this day and every day that we may never walk away from your truth, that we may never run away from your love. We make this prayer in the mighty name of Jesus Christ, Our Lord. Amen.

Dive **Deeper**

Praise God for his faithfulness! Praise God for his eternal love! In prayer, adore God for his fullness of being and beautiful love for you. Ask him to shower you with the grace to accept his love and strengthen your desire to abide in him forever.

Reflect on the **Faith**

- "Everyone is made in the image and likeness of God" (CCC 225).
- If we believe in God, we will not cling to those things that do not help us reach him (see CCC 226).
- Faith inspires us to give thanks. All things, even life itself, are gifts of God. (See CCC 224.)
- "Even when he reveals himself, God remains a mystery beyond words" (CCC 230). As St. Augustine said, "If you understood him, it would not be God" (quoted in CCC 230).
- Since God is our source and origin, and he made us in his image and likeness, we are united. All of us belong to the one human family.
- As St. Nicholas of Flüe prayed, "My Lord and my God, take from me everything that distances me from you." He was asking, if it takes me away from you, take it away from me. "My Lord and my God, give me everything that brings me closer to you" (quoted in CCC 226).
- Often in adversity—or even in abundance—we can be tempted to turn away from the Lord.

Take It to **Prayer**

Father in heaven, we thank you so much. Thank you for this day. We thank you for revealing yourself to us as the God who is, the God who is truth, the God who is love, and the God whom we can trust with our whole being, we can entrust everything we are, we can entrust everything we have, everything we've done, everything we will do. We can entrust our past to you. We can entrust our future to you. In this moment, Lord God, we entrust our present to you. We entrust this present moment. With the hearts that are inside our chests, we give them to you, because you are the only one who is absolutely trustworthy. And so we absolutely trust you in this moment. We make this prayer in the name of Jesus Christ, our Lord. Amen.

Dive **Deeper**

What do you turn to as a substitute for God's love? Challenge yourself to identify specific things that distance you from God and humbly ask him for forgiveness in ever turning away from him.

Reflect on the **Faith**

- God's deepest identity, "his innermost secret," is that he is a communion of Persons—the Trinity—that he "is an eternal exchange of love, Father, Son, and Holy Spirit" (CCC 221).
- "The mystery of the Most Holy Trinity is the central mystery of Christian faith and life" (CCC 234).
- The word "theology" is used for the study of God himself, of his "inmost life"; the "economy" of salvation is the way in which God has acted in the world (see CCC 236).
- The more we know God, the more we understand how he acts. The more we understand how he acts, the more deeply we can know him. (See CCC 236.)
- At the very core of God's identity, he is love.
- He is not only loving in himself—Father, Son, and Holy Spirit—but he has made us in his image and likeness. He has made us for love. He loves each of us, knows our name, and cares about each of us.
- Think of all the people who have never heard of God's love for them. We must never take it for granted.

Take It to **Prayer**

We pray, Father in heaven—you have revealed yourself to us. You have revealed yourself to us through your actions. You have revealed yourself to us through the way in which you have communicated your very life to us. And we ask that you at this moment continue to reveal yourself to us, continue to pour out your divine life into our lives because, God, we're coming to this moment from all these different places, and we ask that you please just meet us where we are. And we know that you can because you are everywhere. You are goodness, you are truth, you are love. And you are here, you are right here. So be here with us now. In Jesus' name, we pray. Amen.

Dive **Deeper**

AN ETERNAL COMMUNION OF PERSONS

Here we see depicted "the central mystery of Christian faith," that God is Father, Son, and Holy Spirit (CCC 234). The Son appears in his glorified humanity, while the Holy Spirit appears as a dove, as at the baptism of Jesus.

Reflect on the **Faith**

- God the Father is revealed by the Son (see CCC 240).
- Because we have the Holy Spirit within us, we have a share in the divine nature. So we are able to call God our Father.
- "By calling God 'Father,' the language of faith indicates two main things: that God is the first origin of everything and transcendent authority; and that he is at the same time goodness and loving care for all his children" (CCC 239).
- Many people have a tough time relating to God as Father because of a broken relationship with their own fathers. The *Catechism* says that God "transcends human fatherhood and motherhood, although he is their origin and standard: no one is father as God is Father" (CCC 239).
- Jesus himself was God "in the beginning," as the Word. He was "with" God and *is* God. (See John 1:1; CCC 241.)
- When one Person of the Trinity acts, all three Persons act.

Take It to **Prayer**

Father in heaven, you have revealed your deepest identity, you revealed yourself to us through your Son and your Holy Spirit. You have called us. You have made us into your adopted children. And you are our adoptive Father. You have shared your nature with us. You have shared your divine life with us. And so we just rejoice in you. We give you thanks; we praise you. May you be glorified, may you be loved not just by others, not just by people throughout the world, but may you be glorified and may you be loved by us this day. We praise you, Father. We love you. Amen.

Dive **Deeper**

If God is neither male nor female, why do we call God "Father" and use masculine pronouns to refer to him?

Here is the simple answer: Jesus revealed God to us as Father. There are many instances in the Gospels where Jesus refers to God as "Father," and when the apostles ask him to teach them how to pray, he responds with the Our Father. To the people of Jesus' day, his calling God "Father" was confusing at best and blasphemous at worst, for it made him the Son of God—that is, divine. Today, some find it confusing and objectionable to speak of God in masculine terms. Nonetheless, the fact remains that Jesus himself revealed God as Father and told his followers to pray to God—and have a relationship with him—as Father.

As the *Catechism* makes clear, God is neither male nor female; he transcends human gender. (Of course, Jesus was male, so the use of masculine pronouns in reference to him is clear.) There are countless examples describing both feminine and masculine "attributes" of God, which communicate his intimate love and gentle care for us. Yet God, through Jesus, directly reveals himself to us as "Father" and invites us to be guided by his discipline, live under his protection, and be embraced by his mercy.

Further reading: C. S. Lewis, "Priestesses in the Church?," *God in the Dock: Essays on Theology and Ethics*; Benedict XVI, general audience address, May 23, 2012; Joseph Cardinal Ratzinger, *Introduction to Christianity*, 130–132; Joseph Cardinal Ratzinger, *Jesus of Nazareth*, 134–142; John 1:12, 20:17; Ephesians 3:14–15.

Reflect on the **Faith**

- As we saw yesterday, in Christianity God reveals himself uniquely as Father.
- His fatherhood is not something that begins when he creates. He is *eternally* Father to the Son.
- In the year 325, the Council of Nicaea clearly defined that Jesus is "consubstantial" with the Father. This teaching was further clarified at the Council of Constantinople in 381.
- At the Council of Constantinople in 381, the Church clarified who the Holy Spirit is (see CCC 245). The Holy Spirit "proceeds from the Father *and the Son*" (see CCC 246).
- The sending of the Spirit reveals in its fullness the mystery of the Holy Trinity.
- The Holy Spirit is active in the Church today.
- In 1054, the Church experienced a schism between East and West, partially over the theological language used to describe the Holy Spirit.
- We continue to pray for a restored full unity with the Eastern Orthodox Church so, as St. John Paul II has said, the Church "may breathe with her two lungs."[4]

Take It to **Prayer**

Father in heaven, you have sent the Holy Spirit through your Son, Jesus Christ, into this world. We ask you, once again, in the name of Jesus Christ, to send your Holy Spirit so that we can understand what it is you wish to reveal to us. We ask you to send your Holy Spirit so that whatever division we experience, not only in our own hearts but also in the Church, in our relationships, and our families—the Spirit of unity will come into those places of brokenness, those spaces of division, and bring wholeness again, bring reconciliation. We pray in a special way for the reunification of the Church, East and West. We pray that once again the Church may fully breathe with both lungs, East and West, maybe even in our lifetimes. Lord God, we ask you this in the name of your Son, Jesus Christ, our Lord, by the power of the Holy Spirit. Amen.

Dive **Deeper**

Pray in special gratitude for the actions of the Holy Spirit in the Church today. Ask God for a strengthened unity of heart, family, community, and Church in your prayers.

Reflect on the **Faith**

- To describe the Trinity, the Church uses certain words from philosophy, such as *substance*, *person*, *hypostasis*, and *relation* (see CCC 251).
- The Church uses these terms to teach that, while God is Father, Son, and Holy Spirit, the Father is not the Son, the Son is not the Holy Spirit, and the Holy Spirit is not the Father.
- The Church uses the words *substance*, *essence*, or *nature* "to designate the divine being in its unity"—there is only one God—while the word *person* (or *hypostasis*) is used to show the "real distinction" between the Father, Son, and Holy Spirit (see CCC 252).
- Every Christian is baptized in the Trinitarian formula—that is, in the name of the Father, Son, and Holy Spirit.
- In the Gospels, it is clear that Jesus claims equality with the Father.
- Each divine Person is the bearer of the divine substance or nature, while the one divine nature is that through which each Person exists and acts.
- It is OK if this language is confusing. With our finite minds, we cannot fully comprehend the infinite mystery that is God.
- God the Father is Father because of the Son, and the Son is Son because of the Father, and the Holy Spirit is the bond of love between them.

Take It to **Prayer**

Father in heaven, we ask you, in the name of your Son, Jesus Christ, to send your Holy Spirit to enlighten our minds, to enliven our hearts. Just please, help us to begin, even just begin to understand, or even capture—help us to take one closer step into the mystery of who you are in yourself. We are nothing without you. We are everything with you. You love everything that is, that we are. You love us infinitely. Help us to know, as deeply as we possibly can, what and who you are, so we can love you and glorify you for what and who you are. In Jesus' name, we pray. Amen.

Dive **Deeper**

If Jesus is divine, why did he pray to God the Father?

The foundational revelation of our Faith is that God is a Trinity of Persons—Father, Son, and Holy Spirit. The three divine Persons live in an eternal communion of love. With this awesome mystery in mind, the question of why Jesus prays to his Father answers itself. As human beings, each of us has a human father. We would not ask someone, "So why do you talk to your father?" I speak to my father because he is my father and I am his child—because we have a relationship. The *Catechism* makes it clear that human beings love and communicate with one another precisely because we are made in the image of God, who is a loving communion of Persons. (See CCC 357, 1702.)

Later in the *Catechism*, we will see what this prayer of Jesus to his Father looked like in detail, but the teaching on the Holy Trinity here shows us how this prayer flows from the profound unity between Father and Son: "The Father is wholly in the Son" and "the Son is wholly in the Father" (CCC 255). Jesus wants us to learn how to pray so that our prayer may come to share in his union with the Father—so that, as he prays, his disciples "may all be one; even as you, Father, are in me, and I in you" (John 17:21).

Key reading: CCC 249–256, 357, 371–373

Reflect on the **Faith**

- The Trinity is one in substance, in essence (see CCC 253). There is only one God.
- The three "*divine persons are really distinct from one another*" (CCC 254).
- All three Persons are distinct because of their relationship with one another—the Father is "Father" in relation to the Son, the Son to the Father (see CCC 255).
- God is love. That is only possible if God is three distinct Persons and yet one divine Being.
- As St. Gregory of Nazianzus writes, "[In the Trinity, there is] divinity without disparity of substance or nature, without superior degree that raises up or inferior degree that casts down ... the infinite co-naturality of three infinites. Each person considered in himself is entirely God" (quoted in CCC 256). The Father is not "more" God than the Son or the Holy Spirit.
- St. Gregory of Nazianzus goes on, "I have not even begun to think of unity when the Trinity bathes me in its splendor. I have not even begun to think of the Trinity when unity grasps me" (quoted in CCC 256). We cannot grasp the Trinity. But the Triune God grasps us.

Take It to **Prayer**

Father in heaven, we praise you and glorify you. We know that you revealed yourself through the Son; you continue to reveal yourself and come to us in the power of the Holy Spirit. You are one God and three divine Persons. And we just ask that you, please, not only help us to see your work in this world and experience your grace in this world but also help us to understand who you are in yourself. Not just in your works, but who you are in yourself. And let this time that we listen to these four paragraphs in the Catechism, *let them just open our minds and open our hearts. Since we know you better, we can love you better. In Jesus' name, we pray. Amen.*

Dive **Deeper**

How can I understand the Trinity better?

The *Catechism* calls the Trinity the "central mystery of Christian faith and life" (CCC 234). The word "mystery" here does not mean a puzzle that we will eventually solve if we think about it long enough. Theologically, a "mystery" is a profound truth that God reveals to us so that we can enter into it. A Christian mystery is a call to step into the world of the divine with trust in God. The world of the Holy Trinity is infinite in terms of the richness and goodness of what we begin to discover. This is why St. Gregory of Nazianzus writes to catechumens that the mystery of the Trinity will be their companion for the whole of their lives (see CCC 256).

The closest we can come to understanding the Trinity is by analogy with knowing another person. While we are always trying to work out how the other person "ticks," we quickly realize that we cannot study a person as if he or she were an object of scientific investigation. If we want to know more, the person will have to freely reveal him or herself to us. And any personal revelation is best understood as an invitation to begin to enter into the mystery of the other person. We renew our pledge to enter more deeply into the mystery of the Trinity every time we make the Sign of the Cross.

Key reading: CCC 234, 253–256, 357

Reflect on the **Faith**

- As we have seen, the word *economy* (*oikonomia*) refers to the order or management of a house—in theological terms, it means the ways in which God has acted in time.
- "The whole Christian life is a communion with each of the divine persons ... Everyone who glorifies the Father does so through the Son in the Holy Spirit; everyone who follows Christ does so because the Father draws him and the Spirit moves him" (CCC 259).
- God has been working in the world from the time of Creation, through the Fall, and through all of salvation history to the present day.
- The three Persons of the Trinity work in unique ways but are always united.
- As St. Elizabeth of the Trinity prayed, "O my God, Trinity whom I adore, help me forget myself entirely so to establish myself in you, unmovable and peaceful as if my soul were already in eternity" (quoted in CCC 260).
- The life of the Trinity dwells inside each one of us because we are temples of the Holy Spirit.

Take It to **Prayer**

Father in heaven, we give you praise and glory. We ask you to please bless this time and guide these next few minutes, that what you have revealed to us through your Church, about your very identity, about your very mission, and about our very ultimate end, may be understood by all of us—so that we can not only apprehend you, not only comprehend you, not only get closer to you but, ultimately, find our home with you forever. In Jesus' name, we pray. Amen.

Dive **Deeper**

THE REVELATION OF THE TRINITY

At Jesus' baptism in the Jordan River, depicted here by Francesco Albani, we have a theophany—a revelation of God that includes the Father in the heavens, the Son baptized by John, and the Holy Spirit coming upon Jesus in the form of a dove (see CCC 258).

Reflect on the **Faith**

- As we have seen, the Trinity "is the central mystery" of our Faith. We can only know that God is one God in three Persons because he revealed this truth to us (see CCC 261).
- There is a sense that when one Person of the Trinity is present, all are present. When one acts, all act, yet in a distinctive way.
- When the second Person of the Trinity took on a human nature in Jesus Christ, he revealed that God is the eternal Father, as he is eternally the Son (see CCC 262).
- The Holy Spirit, "sent by the Father in the name of the Son and by the Son 'from the Father,'... is one and the same God" (CCC 263).
- Ultimately, God wants us to share in his blessed life, in eternity, in heaven.
- The Athanasian Creed proclaims, "We worship one God in the Trinity and the Trinity in unity, without either confusing the persons or dividing the substance ... their glory [is] equal, their majesty coeternal" (CCC 266).
- In this very moment, God exists in glory. His majesty is real and active in this very moment.

Take It to **Prayer**

Father in heaven, we know that we desire to know who you are, and yet you are mystery. We cannot know you fully. But in some ways, we can love you fully. We want to know you more. We want to, even more than know you more, we want to love you more. Help us to know you more so that we can love you more. And above all, Lord God, by your grace, send your Spirit to open our hearts so that we can love you the way you deserve. Send your grace into our hearts that we can love you the way you love us and bring us into your own blessed life, bring us into that relationship where you are Father, Son, and Holy Spirit. We make this prayer in the mighty name of Jesus Christ, our Lord. Amen.

Dive **Deeper**

In prayer, thank God for the mystery of the Holy Trinity. Praise God for his majesty and glory revealed as Father, Son, and Holy Spirit and praise him for his desire to call you to share in the life of the Blessed Trinity.

Reflect on the **Faith**

- God is almighty; he is all powerful. Another word for this is "omnipotence," which is the only divine attribute mentioned in the Creed (see CCC 268).
- God can do whatever he wills. "Nothing is impossible with God, who disposes his works according to his will" (CCC 269).
- As St. Thomas Aquinas notes, "In God, power, essence, will, intellect, wisdom, and justice are all identical. Nothing therefore can be in God's power which could not be in his just will or his wise intellect" (see CCC 271).
- If God is good and almighty, then why does he allow suffering? The presence of pain and evil can make it seem as though God is not there, does not care, or cannot put an end to it (see CCC 272).
- "In the most mysterious way God the Father has revealed his almighty power in the voluntary humiliation and Resurrection of his Son, by which he conquered evil" (CCC 272).
- God's power is absolute but also loving.
- God does not remove suffering; he redeems it.
- The Blessed Virgin Mary set the greatest example of faith, believing that God had the power to do whatever he willed (see CCC 273).
- Once we accept that God's power is universal, God's power is loving, and God's power is mysterious, then there is nothing that we will hesitate to accept in what he reveals about himself (see CCC 274).

Take It to **Prayer**

Father Almighty, you are the almighty Father. You are simple. You are one. Lord God, you are justice and goodness itself. You are being itself. You are love itself. Every good thing flows from you. Every truth flows from you. All of our wills, that can choose and can love, are a gift from you. All of our intellects, that can think and apprehend—they are from you. So, we ask you, Lord, help us to think. Help us to know. Help us to love you. For you are wisdom, and you are love. And we declare that you are good. In Jesus' name we pray. Amen.

Dive **Deeper**

Think of a time when your understanding of God as a loving father was challenged. Did you encounter his forgiveness, fidelity, and joy when you turned to him?

Reflect on the **Faith**

- Science asks, "How and what?" or, "What is this? How did it come to be?" Faith asks, "Who and why?" or, "Who made this? Why was it made?"
- The universe is not some cosmic accident; there is a mind at work—the mind of God, who is the Creator.
- Everything that exists, both visible and invisible, was created *on* purpose *for* a purpose.
- As the *Catechism* says, "Creation is the foundation of 'all God's saving plans,' the 'beginning of the history of salvation' that culminates in Christ" (CCC 280).
- The discoveries of science can help us have a deeper appreciation for creation—and the power of its Creator (see CCC 283).
- Some questions go beyond the domain of the natural sciences, such as those surrounding the meaning and purpose of creation. These questions are crucial for how we live and the choices we make (see CCC 282).
- In a purely material world, there is no such thing as free will, no right or wrong, no objective morality.
- God made heaven and earth; he created all that is visible and all that is invisible.
- This is why there is a world instead of no world; this is why there is something rather than nothing: because God loves us, and he wants each of us to have eternal life with him.

Take It to **Prayer**

Father Almighty, we praise you, and we give you glory. You are the Father Almighty, Creator of heaven and earth, of all things visible and invisible. So we trust in you. We trust you not just because of your power. We trust because we also have asserted, you have revealed that you're not just powerful, you are the Father All-Powerful, you are the Father Almighty, that your power is rooted in love because you are—your deepest identity is love. And so we can trust you. Help us to trust you even more. Lord, help us to open our minds, open our eyes, to be able to see what it is you wish to show us about the beauty of creation and your role as the Creator of heaven and earth, of all things visible and invisible. In Jesus' name we pray. Amen.

Dive **Deeper**

Can a Catholic believe in evolution?

If the term "evolution" means the theory that life on earth developed from random chance or purely "natural selection" (the view of Darwin) with no divine role or direction, then the answer is no.

Scientific evidence does not, in fact, contradict the teachings of the Catholic Faith. As St. John Paul II said, "Truth cannot contradict truth."[5] The Church teaches that God created the universe—including earth and everything in it—from nothing, making mankind in his image and likeness (see Genesis 1:26). God directly created the souls of the first man and woman, from whom all humanity is descended. Science can never contradict the truths God has revealed to us through Christ and his Church. Some theories, which have suggested that God used an evolutionary process to create the world, do not directly contradict revealed truth; however, a Catholic should take into account such factors as the teachings of the Church Fathers, the correct interpretation of Scripture, and the best scientific scholarship when weighing such theories.

As St. John Paul II said, "The sciences of observation describe and measure ... while theology brings out ... ultimate meaning."[6] Legitimate scientific discoveries add to our understanding of details of life on earth, but science cannot account for the meaning of life, the nature of humanity, and the dignity of the human person—much less the role of God as Creator of all. For that, we need divine revelation.

Further reading: "Truth Cannot Contradict Truth," address of St. John Paul II to the Pontifical Academy of Sciences, October 1996; *Gaudium et Spes* 5, 15, 19, 22, 24, 33–36; John Paul II, encyclical letter *Fides et Ratio*; Pius XII, encyclical letter *Humani Generis*

Reflect on the **Faith**

- Ancient religions and cultures have many myths about the origin of the world. Pantheism, Manichaeism, Gnosticism, Deism, and materialism are some of the worldviews that are incompatible with Christianity (see CCC 285).
- God has revealed himself to us in creation, so his existence can be perceived with human reason (see CCC 286).
- From creation, we can discern that God is powerful, that he is outside of the world, and that he is intelligent. The beauty in the world shows us that it is designed. Only a powerful being could create such an awesome creation.
- There is evil in the world, but it is not an eternal force equal and opposite to God. God is all-powerful and fully good.
- One common view among young Americans suggests that God simply wants everyone to be nice, that everyone goes to heaven, and that God stays out of our lives unless we really need something. This view does not describe the God of the Bible or our Faith.
- As the letter to the Hebrews states, "By faith we understand that the world was created by the word of God, so that what is seen was made out of things which do not appear" (Hebrews 11:3; see CCC 286).
- God has revealed everything we need to know (but not every fact there is) about creation.
- God created the world so that we could have a relationship with him.

Take It to **Prayer**

Father Almighty, God all powerful, you are good. You are merciful. You are powerful. You have created all things out of nothing. And you created all things for yourself. You have created us for yourself. You have created this universe for us, to get to know you. To reveal you to us and to bring us closer to you. And so, today, we ask you to please bring us closer to you. Bring us into your grasp. Bring us into your heart, and there we will find joy. In Jesus' name we pray. Amen.

Dive **Deeper**

Have you encountered a beautiful sunset or breathtaking view of nature that led you to praise the Creator? Find something beautiful in nature today, even if it is something small, that showcases the goodness of God's creation, pointing to the hope of our salvation.

Reflect on the **Faith**

- In Genesis 1:1, we read, "'In the beginning God created the heavens and the earth': three things are affirmed in these first words of Scripture: the eternal God gave a beginning to all that exists outside of himself; he alone is Creator ... The totality of what exists ... depends on the One who gives it being" (CCC 290).
- As St. Paul wrote to the Colossians, "In him all things were created, in heaven and on earth ... all things were created through him and for him. He is before all things, and in him all things hold together" (Colossians 1:16–17; see CCC 291).
- St. Irenaeus said, "There exists but one God ... he is the Father, God, the Creator, the author, the giver of order. He made all things *by himself*, that is, by his Word and by his Wisdom" (quoted in CCC 292).
- Why did God create the world? For his glory. Not because he needed anything, nor "to increase his glory, but to show it forth and to communicate it" (CCC 293).
- God creates by his wisdom and by his love. He does not create out of anything other than his goodness, wisdom, and love. He creates freely, out of nothing (see CCC 295–296).
- God gains nothing from our worship; he gains nothing from revealing his glory to us. He does it for our benefit.
- Creation is not a thing of the past. Creation and "re-creation" are happening right now.
- God was able to make the light shine in the darkness by his word when he said, "Let there be light," and he can also give the light of faith to those who do not yet know him.

Take It to **Prayer**

Father in heaven, we thank you and we give you praise. Thank you for revealing yourself to us in these first words of the book of Genesis, and revealing yourself to us—what we need to know about you and what we can know about you by your revelation and by the unfolding of your revelation in our understanding of the history of the Church. Thank you so much. Thank you for those who have gone ahead of us and have figured it out and are passing it on to us today. In Jesus' name, we praise you. Amen.

Dive **Deeper**

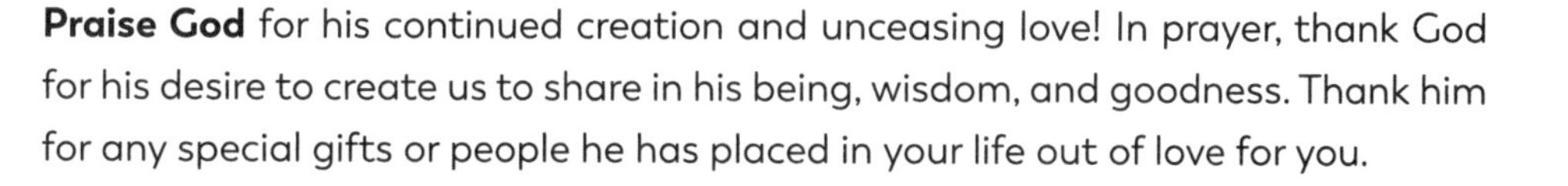

Praise God for his continued creation and unceasing love! In prayer, thank God for his desire to create us to share in his being, wisdom, and goodness. Thank him for any special gifts or people he has placed in your life out of love for you.

Reflect on the **Faith**

- God is good, and he has created a good and ordered world. But he transcends and upholds his creation—and he is always "present to" it (see CCC 300).
- As we read in the Acts of the Apostles, "In him we live and move and have our being" (Acts 17:28; see CCC 300).
- Divine providence refers to God's action in the world. He is the primary cause of all things, but he allows secondary causes in the world. He allows us to act.
- God chose to create us as free beings, with the ability to freely participate in his providence and his plan of salvation for the world. We can say yes to God or no to him.
- Our Father in heaven watches over us, and so Jesus calls us to have a child's trust in his care (see CCC 305).
- We can enter deliberately into the divine plan by our actions, our prayers, and our sufferings.

Take It to **Prayer**

Father in heaven, we thank you. We thank you for this day. We thank you for creating this good world. We know that we broke it. We know that we broke it in our original sin. And you called us to live in this broken world as people with broken hearts. But you have also entered into this broken world. You are immanent. You are present to us. You did not abandon us to the domain of death. For you came in mercy to the aid of all. Come to our aid now, with your mercy, with your love, and with your divine providence. Help us to say yes to you this day and every day. In Jesus' name, we pray. Amen.

Dive **Deeper**

How can you strengthen your childlike abandonment to the heavenly Father? Today, find one way to deepen your faith in him by trusting him to care for his beloved child's specific request.

Reflect on the **Faith**

- How can there be evil in the world since God is all powerful, he made creation good, and he continues to watch over what he has made? Only the entirety of the Christian Faith can address the scandal of evil (see CCC 309).

- God's answer to evil is himself, in the person of his Son, Jesus. He freely allows evil to overwhelm him so that he can conquer and transform it. He doesn't remove evil from the earth, but he redeems it.

- Since we have been granted intelligence and freedom, we must freely seek to be faithful to the moral law. We can also reject it and sin.

- But, as the *Catechism* tells us, "God is in no way, directly or indirectly, the cause of moral evil. He permits it, however, because he respects the freedom of his creatures and, mysteriously, knows how to derive good from it" (CCC 311).

- St. Augustine writes, "'Because he is supremely good, [God] would never allow any evil whatsoever to exist in his works if he were not so all-powerful and good as to cause good to emerge from evil itself" (CCC 311).

- As St. Paul writes to the Romans, "We know that in everything God works for good with those who love him" (Romans 8:28; see CCC 313).

- God is Lord of all the events of history. But we do not always know the details of the divine plan (see CCC 314).

- We get to say yes to God, but we also have the capacity to say no. Because God has created us free, we have the capacity to love. But we also can choose not to love. This is why moral evil—which as the *Catechism* highlights as "incommensurably more harmful than physical evil" (CCC 311)—exists in the world. In his providence, though, God can bring good from evil.

Take It to **Prayer**

Father in heaven, we thank you. In all things we thank you. We know that all things will be well. But, in the meantime, we walk through this valley of the shadow of death. We walk through this vale of tears. So, Lord, we know that not one of our tears falls to the ground without you knowing it. We know that none of us take a step alone without you by our side. But we ask that you please give us just enough light to take that next step. Give us just enough light to be able to trust in you with our whole lives, even in the midst of the valley of the shadow of death. Even in the midst of suffering and brokenness. Even in the midst of our sorrow and grief. We ask you to help us to trust in you. In Jesus' name we pray. Amen.

Dive **Deeper**

God never promised to rid the world of evil, tragedy, and suffering, but he instead promised us hope. Take ten minutes today to watch the Ascension Presents video "'Why Would God Allow This?' Believing in a God Who Allows Evil" and hear from Fr. Mike about the importance of remembering God's faithfulness and his promise to be always present to us even in the midst of pain.

Reflect on the **Faith**

- Today we have a sort of summary of the *Catechism*'s section on creation.
- God did not create the world arbitrarily. He did not create the world because he was bored. God created the world because he is love—and he desired to share his love with free creatures he made in his image and likeness.
- We have been given the opportunity to work together with God's providence (see CCC 323).
- There is a mystery as to why God allows suffering and evil.
- Our "faith gives us the certainty that God would not permit an evil if he did not cause a good to come from that very evil, by ways that we shall fully know only in eternal life" (CCC 324).
- God wants us to share in his truth, his goodness, and his beauty. This is the glory for which he created us.
- Jesus entered into our suffering. He entered into both physical and moral evil. He allowed physical evil to afflict him. He allowed moral evil to crucify him. In his resurrection, he conquered, transformed, and redeemed this evil.
- Though God can bring good out of evil, this in no way makes evil itself good.

Take It to **Prayer**

Father in heaven, we give you praise and thanks. Thank you for continuing to reveal yourself to us. Thank you for continuing to speak to us. Thank you for giving us your Word in Scripture. And thank you for giving us the way to clearly understand your Word through the interpretive lens of the Church and the voice of the Church that continues to speak truth in this world. We thank you. Thank you for creating this world. Thank you for creating us. Thank you for walking with us, even in the midst of our pain and our suffering, our grief, and our loss. We trust in you this day. We love you. In Jesus' name we pray. Amen.

Dive **Deeper**

In prayer, ponder how you can participate in God's truth, goodness, and beauty today. Praise him for the glory for which you were created and ask for continued help in choosing to follow his plan for you in your life.

Reflect on the **Faith**

- We know by faith that angels exist. Scripture and Tradition tell us this. (See CCC 328.)
- What are angels? They are "purely *spiritual* creatures." They "have intelligence and will: they are personal and immortal" (CCC 330). They can know and they can choose.
- As St. Augustine writes, the name "angel" refers to what the angels do. They serve God and bear his messages. (See CCC 329).
- God created angels (spiritual beings) and earthly creatures (material beings). Humans have both a spiritual soul and a material body, which makes us unique in creation. (See CCC 327.)
- Humans do not become angels after death. Humans and angels are different creatures.
- The angels were created to glorify God, and they do. We were also created to glorify God. Only we can glorify God in our bodies.

Take It to **Prayer**

Father in heaven, we love you and we thank you. We know that you have made more than we can see—more than eye can see, more than ear can hear, more than the human heart and mind can understand. You have made all. And we ask you, Father in heaven, to reveal to us the world that you created: The world that is visible—give us eyes to see the world that is visible. And give us the faith to walk in and possess, to understand in a new way, the world that we don't see. You made it all. And you have made it for your glory and to communicate your divine life to us. So Lord God, send our angel to protect us. And hear our prayers through the intercession of every great saint and every angel. In Jesus' name we pray. Amen.

Dive **Deeper**

JACOB'S LADDER

Angels are servants of God; they are his messengers, playing a powerful and constant role in salvation history (see CCC 329). This image shows Jacob's dream, in which angels are ascending and descending a ladder that connects heaven and earth.

Reflect on the **Faith**

- With their whole beings, the angels serve God. They are fully surrendered to the Lord. They belong completely to him. (See CCC 331.)

- Tradition teaches that each of us has a guardian angel. As St. Basil says, "Beside each believer stands an angel as protector and shepherd leading him to life" (quoted in CCC 336).

- We continue to exist because God wills us at every single moment to exist.

- We belong to God because we were created through him and for him. When we do his will, we even more fully belong to him. We are called to live in that place of belonging fully to the Lord.

- Angels have intercessory power, as do the saints. Angels have a double mediation. They bring us the tenderness of God and transmit to us the message of God.

- While still on earth, Christians already live the life of faith in the blessed company of angels (see CCC 336).

Take It to **Prayer**

Father in heaven, we give you praise. We give you praise for the created world, visible and invisible. We give you praise for creating this earth and the heavens. We give you praise for the fact that the heavens are your place, your home. And yet, you are present to us in this place, in our home. Lord God, lead us through this dangerous world by the protection of your grace, by the protection of your angels. Help us to be aware more and more of the unseen world. Help us to be aware more and more of your divine presence in our lives. Help us to be more and more aware of the angelic presence of these creatures, these beings, that love you and serve you and surround us. We make this prayer in the mighty name of Jesus Christ, our Lord. Amen.

Dive **Deeper**

Does every person have a guardian angel?

The Catechism says, quoting St. Basil, "Beside each believer stands an angel as protector and shepherd leading him to life." As human beings, we are both bodily and spiritual, and God provides us not only with bodily companions on earth but with spiritual ones as well. The *Catechism* teaches that from our conception to death these heavenly companions surround us (see CCC 328–336). All angels are spirits with intelligence and will. The word "angel" means "messenger," so guardian angels are God's personal messengers to us who express and enact his loving care and desire for us. The *Catechism* describes our guardian angel's relationship to us as one of protecting and "shepherding" us into life (CCC 336), an image that reminds us that they represent Christ the Good Shepherd.

Jesus does not force us to respond to him; therefore, he does not send his angels to overpower us. They cannot read—or control—our minds. Like them, we are free beings who must choose to reveal ourselves to respond to Christ's love. We must freely cooperate with their protective care. And after we die? Jesus tells us movingly about the joy in heaven of the angels if we do respond to his saving grace and come home to our Father (see Luke 15:1–10).

Key reading: CCC 331–336

Reflect on the **Faith**

- Everything exists because God wills it to exist, and he created out of nothing (see CCC 338).
- Each created thing has "its own particular goodness and perfection" (CCC 339).
- God has made his creatures interdependent on one another. None of us is truly independent of the rest of creation. We all need each other (see CCC 340).
- The six days of creation indicate the "hierarchy of creatures," with the less perfect being created first (see CCC 342).
- "Man is the summit of the Creator's work"; the creation of man is described uniquely in Scripture (see CCC 343).
- God is all-powerful, which means that nothing happens without God directly willing it. Everything falls under God's perfect or permissive will.
- The world reflects God's order. So he does not need to directly cause rain to fall; secondary causes, such as gravity, play a role. Material creation is endowed with its own order and laws.
- We are stewards of the earth, not owners of it. The world is here for our use, not our abuse.
- We are called to use the gifts we have been given in a wise way.

Take It to **Prayer**

Father in heaven, we know that you love us. We know that you are with us. We thank you for this day. We thank you for all you have created, everything invisible and also everything visible, everything we don't see and everything we do see. We thank you because all of it reflects your beauty. All of it reflects your power and your goodness and your love for us. Keep us in your love. Help us to never wander away from it. In Jesus' name, we pray. Amen.

Dive **Deeper**

You were created to reflect God's wisdom and goodness. How can you use your gifts in a wise and meaningful way for the glory of God?

Reflect on the **Faith**

- All of creation—from human beings, made in God's image and likeness, down to minerals, atoms, and even time itself—has been created by God. Everything that exists is meant to give glory to God. (See CCC 344.)
- All of creation, everything that exists, is oriented toward worship (see CCC 347).
- "As the rule of St. Benedict says, nothing should take precedence over 'the work of God,' that is, solemn worship" (CCC 347).
- God entrusted the Sabbath to Israel to keep as a sign of his irrevocable covenant with them. The Sabbath is for the Lord, holy and set apart for the praise of God and his saving actions on behalf of his people.
- Christians worship on Sunday instead of Saturday because it is the day of Christ's resurrection.
- Every time we go to Mass, we enter into the place where time and eternity meet.

Take It to **Prayer**

Father in heaven, we give you praise and thank you. Thank you so much for covenanting yourself to us. For giving yourself to us. For making us your children. For calling us to be part of your family. Lord God, in making us for worship, you have made us for joy. In making us for worship and orienting our lives towards worship of you, you have extended the invitation for us to dwell in your presence. Help us to live each day with you. Help us to live each day for you. Help us to see in this work of creation the invitation to be in relationship with you. Never let us be parted from you. In Jesus' name, we pray. Amen.

Dive **Deeper**

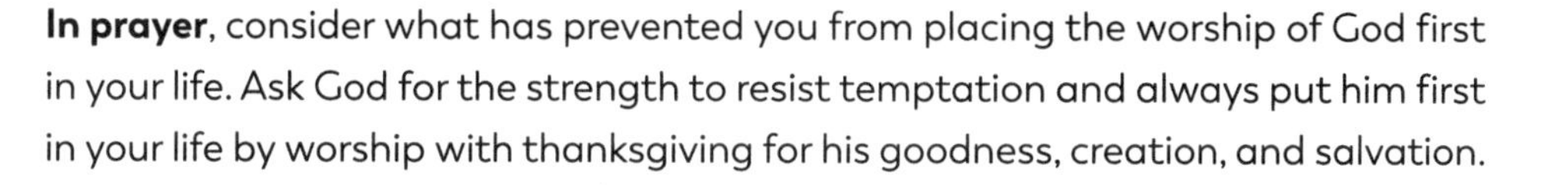

In prayer, consider what has prevented you from placing the worship of God first in your life. Ask God for the strength to resist temptation and always put him first in your life by worship with thanksgiving for his goodness, creation, and salvation.

Reflect on the **Faith**

- Human beings are different from all other creatures, for several reasons: we are made in God's image and likeness; each human being has both a spiritual soul and a physical body; and God created us in friendship with him (see CCC 355).
- We are the only creatures on earth that can choose to love our Creator and the only ones who have been "called to share ... in God's own life" (see CCC 356).
- Humans are capable of self-knowledge. We also are capable of self-possession. We can hold on to ourselves, or we can freely give ourselves away. (See CCC 357.)
- Our dignity means that no one should ever use another human being. We were never meant to be used, only loved.
- We recognize that each of us must respond to God with faith and love. No one can do it for us.
- All human beings, regardless of race, culture, or ethnicity, are united.

Take It to **Prayer**

Father in heaven, we praise you and give you glory. We know that every good thing we have comes from you. We know that every good thing we are comes from you. We know that you have made us free, and you have made us like you. And that is why we are good. We do know that our hearts are broken. We do know that our lives are broken. We do know that our relationships are broken. But we ask that you please, in the midst of that brokenness, help us to see the truth. Help us to see you as you are. Help us to see others as you have made them. And help us to see ourselves, even, in the dignity that you have given us, in creating and redeeming us in your Son, Jesus Christ. We ask this in the name of the same Lord, Jesus Christ. Amen.

Dive **Deeper**

Consider what you can give back to God today. What gifts do you possess from creation that you can offer back to him in a declaration of faith, love, and a gift of self?

Reflect on the **Faith**

- What is a human person? As *Gaudium et Spes* says, "Man, though made of body and soul, is a unity." So a human person is his or her body and soul together (see CCC 364).
- A person's body is "created" by his or her human parents. But an individual's soul is created immediately by God, with no human involvement at all.
- We cannot treat our bodies with contempt. Our bodies are good and must be treated with respect. (See CCC 364.)
- The Church teaches that every soul is created directly by God. The soul is immortal, and it will be reunited with the body at the resurrection of the dead at the end of time.
- There is a temptation to reduce human beings to their bodies alone or to their souls alone—to say either that man is just another animal in this world or that the body is just a trap or cage. But the human person is both soul and body.
- God's plan for salvation included suffering and dying as a man. He took on flesh to be among us and save us.
- The Church teaches that the body and soul are truly one. God does not put someone in the wrong body.

Take It to **Prayer**

Heavenly Father, you have made us in your image and likeness. You have made us soul and body, not that you have a body, God, but that we are in your image. We have intellect and a will. We can choose. We can love. And we give you thanks because not only can we choose and love, we choose and love in our bodies. We also can use our bodies against you. We can use our bodies, we can use our wills, we can use our intellect to reject you or to say no to you. We just ask you, Lord God, keep us entirely yours. Keep us, body and soul, united in love for you. And at that moment, Lord God, at the end of our lives where our body and soul are separated, hold our soul in your hand. Take our soul to you so that one day, in the resurrection of the body, we can be reunited with our bodies, giving you glory for all eternity. We make this prayer in the mighty name of Jesus Christ, our Lord. Amen.

Dive **Deeper**

God made the world—and you—on purpose. Your human body was formed in the image of God and animated by a spiritual soul. Dive deeper into this topic with the Ascension Presents video "Theology of the Body: Why God Gave Us Bodies" and learn from Fr. Mike about the goodness of the human body using the teachings of St. John Paul II's Theology of the Body.

Reflect on the **Faith**

- The Church has always affirmed that men and women are equal in dignity, as human persons, even when this idea has been countercultural (see CCC 369).
- "'Being man' or 'being woman' is a reality which is good and willed by God: man and woman possess an inalienable dignity which comes to them immediately from God their Creator" (CCC 369).
- We always need to remember that we are made in God's image: he is not made in ours. God is not male or female (see CCC 370).
- Men and women are complementary. One cannot bring forth life without the other.
- God has given the earth to human beings to care for.
- If you are married, God has entrusted your spouse to you. If you have been blessed with children, God has entrusted them to you. Our siblings, parents, neighbors—all have been entrusted to us by God.

Take It to **Prayer**

Father in heaven, you have made us male and female. You have made us co-heirs to your life—to your divine life, to the grace that you offer to all human beings. We ask that you come and meet us with that grace. We ask that you come meet us in our maleness. Come meet us in our femaleness. Come meet us in our humanity, because you have made us different, and yet, at the same time, you have imprinted your divine image on every single one of us. So we are equal yet unique and complementary. Lord, help us to appreciate and uphold our equality. Help us to appreciate and honor our complementarity. We ask this in the mighty name of Jesus Christ, our Lord. Amen.

Dive **Deeper**

MAN AND WOMAN IN THE BEGINNING

This image shows God taking Eve from Adam's side. Man and woman are meant to be with one another, as helpmates and friends (see CCC 371).

Reflect on the **Faith**

- God made us for friendship with him. He did not create us simply to exist apart from him but to be in relationship with him.
- The Lord created our first parents in a state of unity with him.
- If Adam and Eve had not sinned but had remained in the state of original holiness, humanity would not have experienced pain or death (see CCC 376).
- The book of Wisdom says, "God did not make death, and he does not delight in the death of the living" (Wisdom 1:13).
- The price of sin is that the harmony, relationship, and intimacy with God that he created us with, and made us for, was broken.
- We experience this brokenness every moment of our lives, but we also experience the incredible gift of God's grace. God enters into our brokenness.
- God has made us for love, for labor, and for leisure.
- Sin can break or twist these things into lust, or drudgery, or idleness.
- When we work, we are collaborating with God in a unique way. Labor, which can be twisted into drudgery or into our identity, can become a good thing that is offered to God.

Take It to **Prayer**

Father in heaven, help us to be your friends. You have made us your children, even though we wander away from you. Even though you have given us every good gift and we turn our backs on you, you have never ceased to call us to yourself. We ask that you please keep calling us. We ask that you please don't just keep calling us but help us to turn back to you, especially in those moments where we want to keep running away from you. You created us for yourself. Help us to be completely yours. In Jesus' name, we pray. Amen.

Dive **Deeper**

Sin breaks our intimacy with God that we were made for. In prayer, ask God for forgiveness for all the times you ran away from him. Thank him for the gift of his grace in entering your brokenness to restore a relationship with him again through his mercy and hope of the resurrection.

Reflect on the **Faith**

- Our Faith teaches us that God is good and that all his creation is good. But each of us experiences the reality of suffering and evil (see CCC 385).
- Moral evil is rooted in sin, which is present throughout human history. We cannot pretend it does not exist. Sin is a rejection of God and his moral law.
- The price of evil is the death of the Son of God. Jesus suffered and died because of sin. This is how far love goes; it reveals the extent of evil and also the superabundance of grace.
- Jesus is the one who reveals to us what it is to have sin and what it is to be redeemed from sin.
- Sin is not just "a developmental flaw, a psychological weakness, [or] a mistake." It is a rejection of God. (See CCC 387.)
- The Church says we cannot fully understand original sin unless we understand, to some degree, grace.
- Even with original sin, we remain good. We are still created in God's image, but we are broken.

Take It to **Prayer**

Father in heaven, we know that you have made this world good. We know that you have made us, human beings, in your image and likeness. You have given us body and soul. You have given us intellect and will. You have given us freedom. You have made us for love. And yet, we so often turn from your love. We so often choose slavery over freedom. Send your Holy Spirit to us right now. Send your Holy Spirit to us wherever we are listening to these words. And we ask you to please unpack not only the reality of sin in our lives but also the devastating reality of sin. Help us to appreciate what sin really is so that we can appreciate the relationship and the friendship we are supposed to have with you. Help us know the darkness, Lord, so that we can know even more fully the light of your grace and the light of your love. And help us to walk in that light. In Jesus' name, we pray. Amen.

Dive **Deeper**

Ponder the devastating damage of your sins. Now, take a few minutes to consider how deep God's love for you is and how strong his superabundance of grace, to redeem your sins by Christ's suffering and death on the cross.

Reflect on the **Faith**

- Before the original sin of Adam and Eve, there was the fall of the angels.
- At one point, some of these spiritual creatures that God made good, that he made to share in his life, rejected him and became evil by their own free choice (see CCC 392). These are the demons.
- Their choice to reject God was made with a full understanding of the consequences. That is why it is "irrevocable" and "unforgivable" (see CCC 393).
- Because they are creatures, the power of the Devil and the other demons is limited (see CCC 395).
- It is a mystery why God allows the Devil to bring about evil and suffering in the world. But we know that God can bring good from it. (See CCC 395.)
- God will not take away our freedom, and he will not take away the freedom of the Enemy.
- St. Peter writes, "Your adversary the devil prowls around like a roaring lion, seeking some one to devour. Resist him, firm in your faith" (1 Peter 5:8).

Take It to **Prayer**

Father in heaven, we know that you are with us. We declare your faithfulness. We declare our trust in your goodness. And we ask for your protection. We ask for your protection against the wiles of the Evil One, against the snares of the Devil. We ask for your protection against all of his lies that can sneak in past our defenses. Lord God, we ask you to please be our guard. You, be our shade against his onslaught. Because you are the one who has conquered Satan. You have conquered death. You have conquered evil by taking death upon yourself and by allowing it to overwhelm you. You have raised it up. You have been raised up. You redeemed us. We know that we trust in you. And we fear nothing. While you are at our side, we fear nothing. We declare this and ask you to be with us in the name of Jesus Christ, our Lord. Amen.

Dive **Deeper**

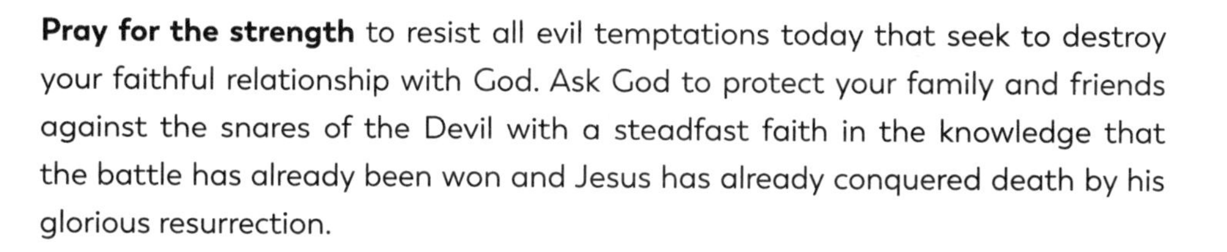

Pray for the strength to resist all evil temptations today that seek to destroy your faithful relationship with God. Ask God to protect your family and friends against the snares of the Devil with a steadfast faith in the knowledge that the battle has already been won and Jesus has already conquered death by his glorious resurrection.

Reflect on the **Faith**

- Our response to God should be, "Father in heaven, I trust you."
- In Genesis 1 and 2, we read that man and woman walked in harmony with God in the Garden; they lived in right relationship with him. They trusted him. They let God love them. (See CCC 396.)
- True freedom is the power to do what we ought to do. But man violated that freedom.
- Tempted by the Devil, our first parents brought death into their souls as they chose not to trust God, disobeying his will (see CCC 397).
- When we sin, we prefer ourselves and our way to God's—which leads us to act against our own good (see CCC 400).
- Before original sin, the first man and woman lived in harmony with creation, with each other, and with God. But now, there is brokenness and death. (See CCC 400.)
- Everyone is now touched by sin.
- God did not abandon us in the midst of our brokenness. In our rebellion and our rejection of him, God did not reject us.

Take It to **Prayer**

Father in heaven, we trust you. We trust you because you did not abandon us to the domain of death. You did not abandon us. You did not let us go in our brokenness. When we rejected you, you did not reject us. You keep on calling out to us. You keep on reaching out for us. Lord God, you sent the prophets. You revealed your Word to us. You revealed your heart to us. You gave us your Son, Jesus Christ, to atone for sin and to show us the way to you, to send us your Holy Spirit. And so, God, we ask you once again, in the name of your Son, Jesus Christ, send us your Holy Spirit, the Advocate, the one who convicts us, the one who leads us into all truth. Lord God, send that Holy Spirit to guide and protect us as we walk forward, talking about sin, talking about the reality of sin, knowing that it's not simply outside of us, but it is truly inside of us. That brokenness is not just around us. It is in our own hearts as well. We ask you to send your Holy Spirit to mend what was broken, to make whole what has been shattered, and to bring back to life what has died. In Jesus' name, we pray. Amen.

Dive **Deeper**

God has never abandoned you, even in the midst of your brokenness and rejection of him. How has God revealed his love for you throughout your life, even during difficult times?

Reflect on the **Faith**

- Due to original sin, human nature lost its original holiness and justice.
- Every one of us is born into this fallen, wounded state. We remain essentially good, but original sin has led to certain consequences. We have an attraction to sin (called *concupiscence*), and we have a darkening of our intellect and a weakening of our will. We suffer and die.
- We can think, but we don't always think clearly. We can choose, but we don't always choose with persistence or perseverance; we don't always choose well.
- Baptism erases original sin. But those consequences are still in us.
- We are fighting against this brokenness in us; we are summoned to a spiritual battle (see CCC 409).
- We are damaged by original sin, but we are not depraved. We are good, but we are broken.

Take It to **Prayer**

Father in heaven, we call upon your name. In the name of your Son, Jesus Christ, we pray. We pray that you continue to meet us with your grace. We pray that you continue to remind us that, yes, we are broken, but we remain beautiful; that we are broken, but we remain good; and that we need you—that you are not optional, Lord God, you are necessary. Your grace is necessary. Without you, we can do nothing. And so, come to our aid. Come with us right now. Come be with us right now. Guide us and give us the strength that on our own we do not have, to be the people that you have created and redeemed us to be. Come, Holy Spirit, give us the divine life, and help us to walk as Jesus walked. In his holy name, we pray. Amen.

Dive **Deeper**

Why does everyone have to suffer the consequences of the sin of Adam and Eve? This seems unfair.

All human persons, of every culture and nation, of every place and time, are created by God in his image and likeness. We are also born with the "stain" of original sin—because we all share in the same weakened human nature. One way of looking at this is that we are all part of the same human family. As with our own families, the decisions and choices of family members can impact everyone—either for good or bad. Similarly, the decision by our first parents to distrust God and disobey him had negative consequences for the rest of the family—for their descendants.

As the *Catechism* states, though we all suffer the effects of the sin of Adam and Eve due to our sharing the same human nature, "the transmission of original sin is a mystery that we cannot fully understand" (CCC 404). While that answer may leave us unsatisfied, it should also leave us with hope. Though we share in the consequences of original sin, we also share access to God's grace and abundant mercy, and eternal life through Jesus Christ, the New Adam, who won salvation for us.

Further reading: Romans 5:18–19

Reflect on the **Faith**

- To live a life of trust and loving obedience to the Father, we have to fight for that trust in ourselves.
- We know that God fights for us. Our Lord's life, death, resurrection, and ascension into heaven are part of that battle for us.
- If we ignore or don't know the fact that we have a wounded nature, then we might think everything that we are inclined to must be good.
- But the full story is that we are made good but broken. We are inclined to evil, and so we have to be on guard even against our own hearts.
- If we forget original sin, then the redemption that was given to us by Jesus Christ is rendered meaningless. But if Christ had not rescued us from slavery to the Evil One, we would be dead in our sins. We can never forget the reality of original sin, and the fact that Christ has transferred us from the power of darkness to his own glorious kingdom through Baptism.
- Knowing this shouldn't cause us to have a negative outlook on life, but we should be prepared for adversity. It gets our hearts ready for the battle.
- Jesus is called the New Adam, and Mary is the New Eve, who obeyed God.

Take It to **Prayer**

Father in heaven, we give you praise and glory. Thank you so much. Thank you so much for bringing us to this day. We ask you to please send your Holy Spirit to enlighten our hearts. Send your Holy Spirit that we can belong to you fully, not just for twenty minutes every day, but to let every minute of every day belong to you, Lord God. We find ourselves in a hard battle, and yet you have not abandoned us in the middle of the battle. You are with us in the midst of this battle, and so we just call out to you. We call upon the name of your Son, Jesus Christ, to send your Holy Spirit to be with us, to guard us, to fight in us and to fight for us. In Jesus' name, we pray. Amen.

Dive **Deeper**

Since Mary was conceived without original sin and one of the consequences of original sin is pain in childbirth, does this mean she had no pain in giving birth to Jesus?

Eve, and every woman down through the centuries who gives birth to a child, gives birth in pain due to original sin (see Genesis 3:16). However, because Mary, the daughter "full of grace" (Luke 1:28) who was chosen to bring the Messiah into the world, was conceived immaculately—that is, without sin (see CCC 490–493)—the long-held theological view is that she did not experience any pain when giving birth to Jesus. This is not a definitive teaching of the Church, though, merely a deduction based on the dogma of the Immaculate Conception. So there is some room for theological questioning and debate about whether Mary experienced pain in childbirth. At the same time, we should acknowledge an abundance of evidence from Scripture, the early Church Fathers, and the Magisterium itself to support the belief that Mary was preserved from the effects of the "curse of Eve."

In the end, we must acknowledge that, because Mary is the new Eve who trusted God's word and obeyed him, it is not hard to believe that God would spare her this particular pain as she brought "salvation in the Flesh" into this world.

Further reading: *Catechism of the Council of Trent*, article 3

Reflect on the **Faith**

- Scripture says we have three enemies: the world, the flesh, and the Devil. This refers to the broken world, our broken human nature, and the Evil One, who wants to get us to rebel against God like he did.
- Every human being is good but also broken. We all have an inclination to sin that we must fight against.
- "The victory that Christ won over sin has given us greater blessings than those which sin had taken from us" (CCC 420).
- Even in the midst of sin, even in the midst of our brokenness, we have hope. Even in our distress, we know we are not abandoned.
- A thief steals because he wants something; a vandal destroys because he does not want someone else to have something. Satan is like a vandal, trying to keep us from the blessings of God.

Take It to **Prayer**

Father in heaven, we know that we can trust you. We know that you do not abandon us to the domain of death. You do not abandon us to the power of the Evil One. We know that we can trust you, even when we say, God, can you just take us out of this situation? Can you remove us from the battle? You don't. Instead, you do something more incredible. You enter into the battle. You didn't take us out of the fight. You enter into the fight. You didn't take us out of suffering. You enter into our suffering. Thank you for being here with us. Thank you for being here with us on this day. And we know that you will be with us every day until that great day when you will be all in all. In Jesus' name, we pray. Amen.

Dive **Deeper**

Are you tired from struggling against evil and temptation in the world? When you are weary, ask God to fill you with a restored strength, rooted in the faith that Christ has triumphed over sin and the knowledge that he will never abandon you.

Reflect on the **Faith**

- We will see how rooted in history the reality of Jesus is. Christianity is a historical religion.
- Jesus was born a Jew, in Bethlehem, under the reign of Herod the Great. He lived in a specific time and place (see CCC 423).
- "Moved by the grace of the Holy Spirit and drawn by the Father, we believe in Jesus and confess, 'You are the Christ, the Son of the living God'" (CCC 424; see Matthew 16:16).
- *Catechism* paragraphs 422 to 424 highlight the good news that God has sent his Son and our response to that good news.
- The next few paragraphs include quotes from *Catechesi Tradendae*, written by St. John Paul II in 1979, to highlight the fact that we need to continue to pass on the Faith. We need to be able to express what we believe and communicate this to other people.
- "At the heart of catechesis we find, in essence, a Person," that is, Christ (CCC 426). "Whoever is called 'to teach Christ' must first seek 'the surpassing worth of knowing Christ Jesus'" (CCC 428).

Take It to **Prayer**

Father in heaven, we give you praise and glory. We thank you so much for sending us your Son. Thank you so much for revealing to us your heart by giving us your Son. Thank you for sending us your Holy Spirit that we can continue to walk as your Son walked. We continue to live as he lived. We continue to love as he loves with the power that comes from you—with the power that comes from the Holy Spirit dwelling inside of us. We ask you, please, help us, not only to know you better and to love you better but help us also to represent you and communicate you, to pass you on better, this day and every day. In Jesus' name, we pray. Amen.

Dive **Deeper**

THE ADORATION OF THE MAGI

The incarnation of Jesus is something radical. God assumed flesh and was born in a particular time and place (see CCC 423). Pictured here is the adoration of the Magi, the wise men who sought out the baby Jesus to bring him gifts as the newborn King and to do him homage.

Reflect on the **Faith**

- The "heart of catechesis" is Jesus Christ, who was a historical person and is the second Person of the Trinity, the only Son of the Father (see CCC 426).
- Whenever we say the name of Jesus, we call upon the Lord God. And he is present with us.
- The name Jesus—in Hebrew, *Yeshua*—means "God saves." "The angel Gabriel gave him the name Jesus as his proper name" (CCC 430), and it has become "the name which is above every name" (Philippians 2:9).
- In chapter 4 of the Acts of the Apostles, we read, "There is no other name under heaven given among men by which we must be saved" (Acts 4:12; see CCC 423).
- Jesus' name is widely abused in our society. We are accustomed to taking the name of Jesus in vain—casually, in anger, or in frustration—even though this is the name through which God has saved us from our sins.
- The Tetragrammaton—*YHWH*, the holy name of God revealed to Moses in the burning bush—was said only once every year by the high priest in the Temple on the Day of Atonement. We underestimate the significance of the name of Jesus.
- As the *Catechism* tells us, "The evil spirits fear his name" (CCC 434). If you ever find yourself in a place of temptation or spiritual battle, prayerfully utter the name of Jesus.
- One way to pray without ceasing in the Eastern Church is the Jesus Prayer: "Lord Jesus Christ, Son of the living God, have mercy on me, a sinner." The name of Jesus actually is a prayer.
- Let the name of Jesus be on our lips and in our hearts—a prayer that permeates our day with every breath.

Take It to **Prayer**

Father in heaven, we know that you have revealed your Son. You have given your Son to us. And your Son has revealed you because he is the image, the perfect image of the Father. Lord God, we trust in your Son, Jesus Christ. We call upon his name. We make our prayer in his name. We ask that you please, through the work of Jesus Christ, your only Son, we ask that you please send us your Holy Spirit that we can truly have a real sense of reverence and awe for your being, of course, but also for your very name. Let the name of Jesus always be on our lips. Let the name of Jesus be tattooed upon our hearts. Let the name of Jesus always be closely present and guide our lives. Lord God, we make this prayer in the mighty name of Jesus Christ, our Lord. Amen.

Dive **Deeper**

Let the divine name of Jesus Christ be in your prayer, on your mind, and in your heart throughout this day. When you find yourself in a place of temptation, remember to prayerfully utter the name of Jesus Christ, who is always present to you.

Reflect on the **Faith**

- "The word 'Christ,' comes from the Greek translation of the Hebrew *Messiah*, which means 'anointed'" (CCC 436). Jesus is the Anointed One (see CCC 438).
- "Christ" is a title that "became the name proper to" him (CCC 436). Many people were anointed in the Old Covenant—kings, prophets, priests. Yet Jesus "accomplished perfectly the divine mission that 'Christ' signifies" (CCC 436). Jesus is the great High Priest, the King of Kings, the fulfillment of all prophets—the messianic hope of Israel.
- Jesus is deeply rooted in the history of the people of Israel. God himself entered into covenant with them. It is from the Jewish people that our salvation, Jesus Christ, comes.
- As St. Irenaeus of Lyons says, "For the name 'Christ' implies 'he who anointed,' 'he who was anointed' and 'the very anointing with which he was anointed.'" This refers to the Holy Trinity: Father, Son, and Holy Spirit. (See CCC 438.)
- Jesus reveals that his being priest, prophet, and King completely transcends mere political power.
- Jesus accepts the title of Messiah only when it is absolutely clear that he is the King crowned with thorns, the High Priest who is himself the sacrifice, the prophet who is rejected.
- Jesus extends a share in his role as priest, prophet, and King to every Christian. He reveals the true meaning of his kingship when he is raised high on the cross. As King, he is also the Suffering Servant.

Take It to **Prayer**

Father in heaven, we give you praise, and we thank you so much. We thank you for sending us your Son. You love the world so much that you gave us your only begotten Son, so all those who call upon his name, all those who believe in him, would not perish but would have eternal life. Now, God, help us to call upon his name. Help us to see that Jesus is the Christ, that he is the Messiah, that he is the Anointed One, that he is the fulfillment of being the priest, the prophet, and the King. And he calls us not only to share in his own divine life, but he calls us to share in the exercise of that three-fold role, that three-fold ministry of priest, prophet, and King. Help us this day and every day to say yes to you and your Son, Jesus, in the power of the Holy Spirit. Amen.

Dive **Deeper**

JESUS IN THE SYNAGOGUE OF NAZARETH

This icon shows Jesus reading in the synagogue of Nazareth. He is manifesting himself as the Christ, or Messiah, who would usher in the messianic age with signs and wonders (see CCC 438).

Reflect on the **Faith**

- The title "son of God" applies to Jesus in a unique way, unlike the ways it was used for others in the past.
- Jesus never prays with the words "our Father," but he tells the disciples to do so. His relationship with the Father is different from theirs because he is the eternal, divine, only begotten Son of God.
- "Only in the Paschal mystery can the believer give the title 'Son of God' its full meaning. After his Resurrection, Jesus' divine sonship becomes manifest in the power of his glorified humanity" (CCC 444–445).
- John 1 says, "In the beginning was the Word, and the Word was with God, and the Word was God ... And the Word became flesh and dwelt among us" (John 1:1, 14).
- John also says, "We have beheld his glory, glory as of the only-begotten Son from the Father" (John 1:14; see CCC 445). This is what the apostles bore witness to—the glory of the only Son of God.
- The one in whom we place our faith and the one to whom we direct all of our love and all of our lives is the only Son, sent from the Father.

Take It to **Prayer**

Father in heaven, in the name of your Son, Jesus—in Jesus, the only Son of God—we ask that you send your Holy Spirit to enter our minds, to penetrate our hearts, so that we can know you more clearly, so that we can love you more accurately and love you more fully. Lord God, we entrust ourselves to you because we know that, in time, you revealed yourself as the one who saves. In time, you revealed the Anointed One, priest, prophet, and King. You revealed yourself in your Son, Jesus Christ, the only Son of the Father. And then by sending your Holy Spirit to us, you allowed us to participate in his divine sonship. You have allowed us to participate in his being able to cry out, "Abba, Father." And so today we do. You have made us, who have been baptized, your children. So you are our dad, and we cry out to you today, "Father, hear our prayer." In the name of Jesus, in the name of the Father, and of the Son, and of the Holy Spirit. Amen.

Dive **Deeper**

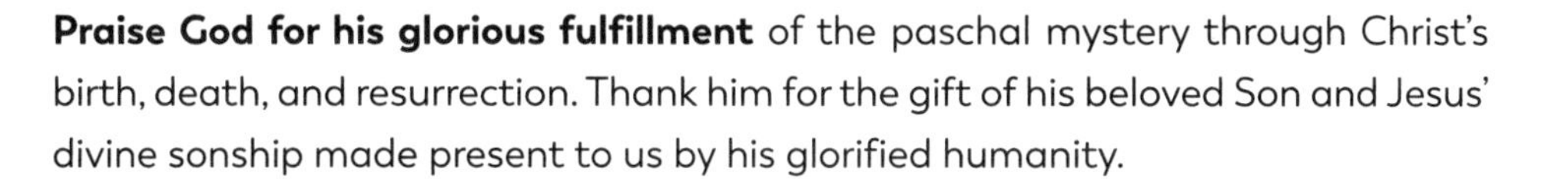

Praise God for his glorious fulfillment of the paschal mystery through Christ's birth, death, and resurrection. Thank him for the gift of his beloved Son and Jesus' divine sonship made present to us by his glorified humanity.

Reflect on the **Faith**

- The holy name of the Lord God revealed to Moses in the burning bush is YHWH. In Greek, this is translated *Kyrios*, which means “Lord” (see CCC 446).
- This was not a mere claim; Jesus “demonstrated his divine sovereignty by works of power over nature, illness, demons, death, and sin” (CCC 447).
- When we say “Jesus is Lord,” we are saying he has lordship over our lives.
- To be a Christian, one must believe that Jesus Christ is the Son of God. What we profess is what the Church professes.
- “Christian prayer is characterized by the term ‘Lord’” (CCC 451), and it highlights the reality that Jesus is Lord.
- As St. Paul wrote to the Corinthians, “No one can say ‘Jesus is Lord’ except by the Holy Spirit” (1 Corinthians 12:3; see CCC 455).
- We are called to let the Lord be our Lord—to give him divine sovereignty over every aspect of our lives, past, present, and future.

Take It to **Prayer**

Father in heaven, we praise and glorify you. We do declare in the power of your Holy Spirit that Jesus Christ is Lord. He is Lord of the living. He is Lord of all. He is Lord who has given himself so fully that all things have been placed under his feet. It's only by the power of the Holy Spirit that we get to say Jesus is Lord. And so we declare, together, as this Catechism in a Year *community we declare that Jesus is Lord to the glory of God the Father now and always. Amen.*

Dive **Deeper**

DOUBTING THOMAS

This famous artwork by Caravaggio shows Thomas touching the wound marks of the Risen Christ. Thomas proclaims, "My Lord and my God!" For Thomas, as for the other apostles, Jesus was Kyrios, *Lord and Master. (See CCC 448).*

Reflect on the **Faith**

- Jesus became flesh for the whole world, but it is important that we recognize that it is concrete and personal. He became flesh for each of us.
- Original sin divided our own hearts, divided us from each other, and divided us from God. Jesus became man to reconcile us to God, that we may be saved (see CCC 457).
- As St. Gregory of Nyssa writes, "Closed in the darkness, it was necessary to bring us the light" (quoted in CCC 457).
- John 3:16 tells us that "God so loved the world that he gave his only-begotten Son, that whoever believes in him should not perish but have eternal life" (see CCC 458). We often hear the truth that God loves us but fail to accept it.
- God loves us so much that he allows us to share in his divine nature. Through the power of Baptism, we became a new creation, adopted by God the Father. He is our Father, and we are his children.
- Great saints have proclaimed that the Son of God became the Son of Man so that men might become sons of God. Jesus became human so that we could be "sharers in his divinity" (CCC 460).
- In St. Paul's letter to the Philippians, we read that Jesus, though still fully God, emptied himself and became one of us. He took on a body so that he could sacrifice himself, to do the Father's will. (See CCC 461–462; Philippians 2:6–8; Hebrews 10:5–7.)
- It has been the Church's joyous conviction, from the beginning, that Jesus was manifested in the flesh (see CCC 463).

Take It to **Prayer**

Father in heaven, we love you. More powerfully than we could ever love you, you love us. More truly than we could ever choose you, you have chosen us. And more faithfully than we could ever be faithful to you, you have laid a claim on our lives. And you have promised yourself, you have covenanted yourself, to us that becoming one of us and even not abandoning us, by even taking our humanity with you into heaven, by taking our humanity into your divinity, Lord God, you have united forever humanity and divinity, and you have even given us a share in your divinity. So Father, I cannot even begin to thank you. I cannot even begin to understand the depth of your love, the depth of your faithfulness. Help us grasp a little bit more clearly today so that we can love you even more truly, today and forever in heaven. In Jesus' name, we pray. Amen.

Dive **Deeper**

Reflect on the truth that the Word became flesh to make us partakers of his divine nature. The Son became incarnate to reconcile us to the Father so that we may be saved. How does this knowledge deepen your desire to know and love God?

Reflect on the **Faith**

- The first heresies were challenges to the understanding of who Jesus truly is. Some claimed that Christ only appeared to be human. Then the Nestorian heresy claimed Jesus was both a human person and a divine person.
- The Council of Ephesus proclaimed that Mary is truly the *Theotokos*, the Mother of God. She is truly the Mother of God because the One who was conceived in her womb was truly the Son of God, who became man at this point in time. This divine Person joined his divine nature to a human nature, which is remarkable.
- Then the Monophysite heresy claimed that when the Son joined his divine nature to a human nature, the human nature ceased to be.
- So the Church had to clarify that Jesus is one divine Person with two natures, human and divine. That is very important. The Council of Chalcedon in AD 451 confessed that truth.
- "One and the same Christ, Lord, and only-begotten Son, is to be acknowledged in two natures without confusion, change, division, or separation. The distinction between the natures was never abolished by their union" (Council of Chalcedon; quoted in CCC 467).
- The Roman Liturgy says that "what he was, he remained": he was God, divine. And "what he was not, he assumed": he assumed humanity (CCC 469).

Take It to **Prayer**

Father in heaven, we know that you have given us your only begotten Son. We know that, in Jesus Christ, one divine Person, there were two natures, human and divine. In so many ways, we don't know how—the details. In so many ways, we don't know exactly what that means. Father, we ask you to help us to understand how your eternal only begotten Son entered into time and entered into our world, in this life, in a unique way, in a unique way in the Incarnation. Help us to understand it just more deeply today so that we can love you and rejoice and give you praise and glory for what you have done in our lives and in the life of every human being. By uniting your divinity to our humanity, you have forever changed our humanity. And we thank you. Help us to live like this this day and every day. We make this prayer in Jesus' name. Amen.

Dive **Deeper**

How should we understand the title "Mother of God"?

The Council of Ephesus in AD 431 affirmed that Mary is *Theotokos*, meaning "God bearer"—she is the Mother of God. Mary is not just the mother of Jesus' human nature; one does not give birth to a "nature" but to a "person." She is rightly called "Mother of God" because Jesus, though possessing human and divine natures, is a divine *Person*, who became incarnate through Mary.

Some non-Catholics misunderstand this title. Though born without original sin, Mary was a human being, not in any way divine. Any charge that Catholics worship her is false. As the Catechism explains,

> The Church rightly honors "the Blessed Virgin with special devotion. From the most ancient times the Blessed Virgin has been honored with the title of 'Mother of God,' to whose protection the faithful fly in all their dangers and needs. . . . This very special devotion . . . differs essentially from the adoration which is given to the incarnate Word and equally to the Father and the Holy Spirit, and greatly fosters this adoration" (CCC 971).

The Son of God chose to become man and be born of a human mother, Mary, for the salvation of the world. By faith in God's revelation, we know that Mary was a virgin who consented to become the Mother of God through the power of the Holy Spirit. Thus Jesus is biologically the son of Mary; he took his human flesh from her. Jesus is truly the Son of God and the son of Mary.

Reflect on the **Faith**

- In Christ, "human nature was assumed, not absorbed." It was not overridden. Jesus had a human intellect, will, and body. (See CCC 470.)
- It is in his human body that Jesus conforms his will to the will of the Father. He assents intellectually and with everything he is to the Father's will.
- There is nothing that Christ did not assume of human nature, except our sinfulness—he was like us in all things but sin.
- Jesus is the Son of the Father, the second Person of the Trinity. He receives the Father's love and pours himself back out in love to the Father. That love is the Holy Spirit, the third Person of the Trinity.
- Jesus in his human soul has the operations of a human intellect and will, the ability to choose, learn, and grow. At the same time, his human intellect is united with his divine intellect, his divine nature (see CCC 472).
- In the Incarnation, the divine Son of God did not "absorb" humanity but took on a human nature—thinking with a human mind, acting with a human will, loving with a human heart—but consistently obedient to the Father. In this, Jesus Christ redeems humanity.
- Jesus could say, "He who has seen me has seen the Father" (John 14:9) because from eternity—even when he assumed human nature—he is the second Person in the Trinity, the Son of the Father.
- With his divine wisdom, Jesus "enjoyed in his human knowledge the fullness of understanding of the eternal plans he had come to reveal" (CCC 474).
- Jesus embraced suffering, knowing fully what would happen to him. In taking on a human nature, he knew he would be rejected and despised.

Take It to **Prayer**

Father in heaven, we thank you. We thank you for the mystery—as confusing as it might be—the mystery of the incarnation of your Son Jesus Christ, that second Person of the Trinity, the Word that became flesh and dwelt among us. And we saw his glory, the glory as of the Father's only Son because, Father, you so loved the world that you gave your Son so that everyone who believed in him might not perish but might have eternal life. Today, help us to know more and more about your Son. Help us today to accept him even more fully. Help us today to be loved by him and to receive that love as we are loved by you and receive your love. In Jesus' name, we pray. Amen.

Dive **Deeper**

How did Jesus' human nature express his divinity?

God has actually taken on the full reality of human life in the incarnation of Jesus of Nazareth. As the *Catechism* says, "Christ ... expresses humanly the divine ways of the Trinity" (CCC 470). Jesus is what, in human terms, God's own life looks like.

The humanity assumed by God the Son is both a sign and an instrument. All that God the Son did shows us something of the life of the Trinity. In addition, the human nature of the Son of God is an instrument to express God's saving love and power. We also see in this part of the *Catechism* that the sacraments Christ instituted and entrusted to the Church are his continuing "signs" and "instruments" of grace (see CCC 774).

Jesus possessed a perfect human nature, one uncorrupted by original sin. On earth, Jesus was "in every respect ... tempted as we are, yet without sinning" (Hebrews 4:15). He did not sin, because his human and divine wills were perfectly united; he was always obedient to the Father's will. Does Jesus' sinlessness make him less than fully human? No, because God never intended sin to be part of our true humanity; it is a bondage that our first parents freely chose. True human freedom is freedom from sin. Jesus' resistance, in the flesh, of every temptation is the expression of perfect human life. In heaven, by God's grace, we will be unable to sin—and therefore truly free at last.

Key reading: CCC 464–478, 515–518

Reflect on the **Faith**

- The iconoclast heresy claimed there could be no images. Yet, because God truly became man, the human face and body of Jesus can be depicted (see CCC 476).
- To answer the iconoclasts, the Second Council of Nicaea in the year 787 proclaimed that in venerating an icon, a person is venerating not the image but the one who is portrayed (see CCC 477).
- It was not the Father on his own sending the Son to die for the sins of humanity. It was the Father, Son, and Holy Spirit united.
- Jesus knew and loved us during his life, agony, and Passion without exception. Before we even came into being, Jesus loved us as he walked this earth—and gave himself up for us.
- "The Sacred Heart of Jesus, pierced by our sins and for our salvation, 'is ... considered the chief sign and symbol of that ... love with which the divine Redeemer continually loves the eternal Father and all human beings' without exception" (CCC 478).
- St. Paul, who never encountered Jesus until Jesus spoke to him on the road to Damascus, still said, "The Son of God ... loved me and gave himself for me" (Galatians 2:20; see CCC 478).
- When we encounter God's love, it becomes intensely personal.

Take It to **Prayer**

Father in heaven, I thank you. I thank you so much for every person who has joined us, every person who pressed play today. This is their day 68. This is our day 68 together. Whether this is the actual day 68, or whether we are struggling to press play every single day, Lord God, this is the day you want us to hear these words. This is the day that you want us to reflect on this truth. This is the day that you want to reveal to our minds the power of knowing you more deeply, so we can love you more truly. Help us to do both. Help us to follow you. Help us to belong to you. Help us to be yours this day, and every day. In Jesus' name, we pray. Amen.

Dive **Deeper**

TRUE GOD AND TRUE MAN

This icon shows Christ as Pantocrator, as Lord and ruler of all. Often holy images of this kind will use colors like red to symbolize Christ's true humanity (and his Passion), and blue or gold to symbolize his divinity. (See CCC 477).

Reflect on the **Faith**

- God has created every person with a destiny—to have eternal life with him forever in heaven, but also to say yes to him on earth.
- God created Mary for a particular mission and destination. She was predestined. But she still had a free choice to say yes to the Lord.
- A long line of holy women in the Bible prepared the way for Mary. They prefigured what Mary would ultimately do in the New Covenant, bringing Jesus into the world (see CCC 489).
- Adam and Eve sinned and handed original sin on to all of humanity. But Mary gave her yes to God, obeyed, and gave birth to the Son, who brought freedom and redemption to the world.
- What we believe about Mary is based on what we believe about Jesus. Mary is truly the Mother of God, the *Theotokos.*
- God prepared a body for himself. From the very moment of his conception, the person in the womb of the Virgin Mary was fully God and fully man.
- The Church's teachings, sacraments, moral life, and prayer all lead us back to God and closer to him.
- Without Mary's yes, we would not have Christ Incarnate, the Messiah.
- God was not too proud to make salvation dependent upon the yes of a simple girl from Nazareth. We cannot be too proud to turn to her and learn from her.
- From the cross, Jesus said to John, "Behold, your mother," and John took her into his home (John 19:27). We, too, are called to take Mary into our homes.

Take It to **Prayer**

Father in heaven, we trust in you. Father in heaven, we call upon your Holy Spirit that came upon the Blessed Virgin Mary and she conceived your Word made flesh in her womb. Send that Holy Spirit in the name of your Son, Jesus Christ, into our lives, that we can be fruitful, that we can say yes to your call, that we can—even when we don't know what it is you are calling us to, that we can say yes to you, the one who is calling us. Help us to have the courage of Mary, the humility of Mary, and the joy of Mary to say yes to you, that your will may be done in our lives this day and every day. In Jesus' name, we pray. Amen.

Dive **Deeper**

What can you learn from Mary's simple but profound yes to the Lord's call? How does Mary's courage, humility, and obedience to the Lord inspire you to say yes to God's plan for you in your life?

Reflect on the **Faith**

- Mary was immaculately conceived. From the very first moment of her existence, she was preserved from original sin (see CCC 490–491).
- This is the dogma of the Immaculate Conception, proclaimed by Pope Pius IX in 1854 (see CCC 491).
- She was preserved from sin by a "singular grace and privilege" from God and by the merits, in advance, of her Son's life, death, and resurrection (see CCC 491).
- Jesus is the new Adam, who gives us life and redemption.
- Mary is the new Eve, without sin, who in obedience gives birth to the eternal Son of the Father.
- The Church Fathers proclaimed that "the knot of Eve's disobedience was untied by Mary's obedience" and that we have "death through Eve, life through Mary" (CCC 494).
- God gave Mary what she needed to accomplish her mission. Mary gave her full consent to become the mother of Jesus. There was no sin that held her back. (See CCC 494.)
- God has created each of us for a mission, a vocation. And he never calls us to something that he does not also give us the grace and power to accomplish.
- Our call is to say, like Mary, "I am the servant of the Lord. Let it be done to me according to your word."

Take It to **Prayer**

Father in heaven, we thank you. In the name of your Son, Jesus Christ, please send your Holy Spirit. As you sent your Holy Spirit within the womb of the Blessed Virgin Mary to bring forth new life, we ask that you please send your Holy Spirit into our lives. Heal what has been wounded in our lives. Fill what has been emptied. Lord God, we ask you to make a space in our lives for you, for your truth, for your will, for your mission. We know, Lord God, that you called Mary, you created her for a mission. And you gave her everything she needed to accomplish that mission. We trust in you that you will do the same for us. That you have created us for our mission and that you will give us everything that we possibly could ever need for that mission. We trust in you, and we pray to you, and we give you glory this day and every day. In Jesus' name, we pray. Amen.

Dive **Deeper**

Since Scripture says that "all have sinned and fall short of the glory of God" (Romans 3:23), how could Mary be sinless?

As the Catechism explains, Mary "was redeemed from the moment of her conception" (CCC 491). In contemplating how Mary could have been sinless, we must remember that she needed a Savior, too. Due to the sin of Adam and Eve, every human being other than Mary is conceived with original sin. Without the grace that comes from being baptized into Jesus, the life of saving grace would remain closed to us. Whereas original sin is washed away from our souls in Baptism, Mary was preserved from original sin by the merits that Jesus would soon win on the cross. As the Catechism says, she was "redeemed, in a more exalted fashion, by reason of the merits of her Son" (CCC 492).

From the earliest days of the Church, Christians believed that Mary was without sin. Mary needed a Savior, but as Pope Pius IX proclaimed when he declared the dogma of the Immaculate Conception in 1854, "the most Blessed Virgin Mary was, from the first moment of her conception, *by a singular grace and privilege of almighty God and by virtue of the merits of Jesus Christ*, Savior of the human race, *preserved* immune from all stain of original sin" (CCC 491; emphasis added). So Mary was preserved from the stain of original sin, and remained free from any personal sin, to be a perfect dwelling for the Son of God.

Further reading: Joseph Cardinal Ratzinger, *Introduction to Christianity*, 203–2011; Pius XI, encyclical letter *Lux Veritatis*

Reflect on the **Faith**

- When Mary visits her, Elizabeth recognizes and proclaims that Mary is the mother of the Lord (see CCC 495).
- The conception of Jesus was supernatural. "Jesus was conceived 'by the Holy Spirit without human seed,'" when the power of the Holy Spirit overshadowed Mary (CCC 496). This conception "surpasses all human understanding and possibility" (CCC 497).
- There has often been a misunderstanding of—and even opposition to—the miraculous conception of Jesus. Yet it was recounted by the apostles because it was true (see CCC 498).
- The three greatest events in the history of humanity were "worthy of proclamation" but "accomplished in God's silence": Mary's virginal conception of Jesus, the birth of Jesus, and Jesus' suffering and death on the cross (see CCC 498).
- The Church confesses that Mary was perpetually a virgin. She is the Mother of God, but "Christ's birth 'did not diminish his mother's virginal integrity but sanctified it'" (see CCC 499).
- Jesus did not have other siblings. When Scripture speaks of James and Joseph as "brothers of Jesus," it is actually speaking of relatives of Jesus who were children of a different woman named Mary (see CCC 500).
- Jesus entrusted Mary to us as our mother. She is the mother of all whom Jesus came to redeem (see CCC 501).

Take It to **Prayer**

Father in heaven, we praise you and give you glory. We thank you so much for bringing us to this day. We thank you for continuing to just illuminate our minds and open up a path before us. We know, Lord God, that your Word is a lamp unto our steps and light unto our path. We know that your Word is in Sacred Scripture. And also your Word is that Second Person of the Trinity, the Word become one of us. We know that our Lord God, you Lord God, light our way in the midst of darkness, whether that be darkness of not understanding, darkness of confusion, darkness of difficulty, darkness of suffering and grief—Lord God, you continue to light our way. Walk with us today and guide us today. Be the lamp unto our feet today. In Jesus' name, we pray. Amen.

Dive **Deeper**

Why was Mary's perpetual virginity necessary?

Belief in the perpetual virginity of Mary has been constant since the earliest days of the Church. This belief was defended in the writings of the Church Fathers and established in the Church's proclamations and liturgy. It is an essential part of Sacred Tradition. But why was it so important that Mary remained a virgin all her life?

Mary's perpetual virginity is a sign of the beauty and abundant fruit God can bring from great sacrifice. Mary's *fiat* to the archangel Gabriel signified a complete gift of herself, a consecration to God, and a promise to love and protect the child Jesus and to follow him, even to the foot of the cross.

A beautiful hymn in the Byzantine Liturgy of St. Basil prays to Mary as "Sanctified Temple and Rational Paradise ... He made your womb a throne, setting it apart, a room more spacious than the heavens."[7] Mary is set apart, her whole life given to God, and her womb is a "throne" for the Son of God that no mere human could worthily inhabit ever after.

Further reading: *The Protoevangelium of James*; decrees of the Second Council of Constantinople (AD 553); Second Vatican Council, *Lumen Gentium*, 56–57; Byzantine hymn, "In You, O Woman Full of Grace"

Reflect on the **Faith**

- Mary is an image of the Church, freely and fully receiving the grace of the Lord (see CCC 507).
- Whatever we believe about Mary are things we believe about Jesus. What we teach about Mary, illumines what we believe and teach about Jesus.
- Jesus is the new Adam, and "from 'his fullness' as the head of redeemed humanity 'we have all received, grace upon grace'" (CCC 504).
- Through the Church, we are conceived by the Holy Spirit in Baptism and born to God to a new and immortal life.
- In Revelation, chapter 12, we see the sign of woman giving birth to a child, which symbolizes Mary's giving birth to Jesus.
- Mary represents the Church: she brought forth the Son of God into the world, and, likewise, through the Church, the Son of God comes into the world.

Take It to **Prayer**

Father in heaven, we give you praise. We love you, and we thank you. We thank you for the mystery of the Incarnation. We thank you for the mystery of the Immaculate Conception of the Blessed Virgin Mary. And we thank you for making us your adopted children. We ask that you, please, just like for Mary, you gave her everything she needed for her mission, we ask that you, please, remember to give everything that we need for our mission. And give us the trust, give us the faith to count on you, to know that you have not and will not ever abandon us but you will always provide exactly what we need. Give us this day our daily bread. Give us this day everything we need and help us to use it. Help us to use it for your glory according to your purposes and according to your will. In Jesus' name, we pray. Amen.

Dive **Deeper**

MARY, THE MOTHER OF GOD

Here we see Mary with the Christ child. Because Jesus is God, Mary is the Mother of God (see CCC 509). As Jesus is the new Adam, so Mary is the new Eve, joining herself in an unparalleled way to the saving mission of her Son.

Reflect on the **Faith**

- Jesus reveals the Father in everything he does (see CCC 516).
- All the details about Jesus that the Gospels mention are included to help reveal him (see CCC 515).
- Jesus enters into the depth of what we experience as human beings, redeems it, and brings it back to life.
- Jesus lived his life for us. He is our example. By his grace, he enables us to imitate him. (See CCC 521.)
- "We are called only to become one with him, for he enables us as the members of his Body to share in what he lived for us in his flesh as our model" (CCC 521).
- Salvation is not just God redeeming us and giving us access to the Father, but also making us capable of living as Christ, to participate in the mysteries that Jesus won for us.

Take It to **Prayer**

Father in heaven, we praise you. Father, first of all, let our praise go up before you. Let our thanksgiving go up before you, Father. Please, in the name of your Son, Jesus Christ, receive our thanks. Receive our praise. You are the eternal God. You are the eternal Father who sent the eternal Son into this world. And his whole life is a revelation of you, of your heart, of your will, of who you are, the depths of your identity. His whole life is a work of redemption, redeeming every aspect of our lives. And his whole life is a recapitulation, where he shows us how we can live in obedience, how we can live trusting, and how we can live in love. Lord God, help us to participate in this. Help us to receive that Holy Spirit, the Holy Spirit sent from you, into our hearts, so that we can live the mystery of Jesus Christ every day in every moment of our lives. In his name, we pray. Amen.

Dive **Deeper**

What do we know of Jesus' life between the age of twelve and the start of his public ministry?

The Bible—apart from discussing his birth and his dialogue in the Temple with the teachers of the law at age twelve (see Luke 2:41–52)—is largely silent about Jesus' life before his public ministry. So there are many things we would love to know! The *Catechism*, though, refers to the details of Jesus' childhood and young adulthood as things merely "of interest to human curiosity" (CCC 514). This period of Jesus' life, which constitutes most of his time on earth, is known as his "hidden life." Of course, we know that he lived in Nazareth with Mary and Joseph, that he was part of the life of his community, and that he lived as an observant Jewish man, obedient to God's law.

Jesus was truly man, "yet without sinning" (Hebrews 4:15), and the hiddenness and obscurity of his life is the pattern of nearly every human life. Only a limited number of people usually know the intimate details of our lives. The wonderful thing about the humility of Jesus in his incarnation is that, by living this hidden life, he has sanctified and made precious all the elements of ordinary daily life. The life of the family, with its chores and basic care of all the necessities of life, the life of work, the patterns of ordinary duty and obedience—all this Jesus has shared in and made holy. So this can be where our daily sanctification can take place.

Key reading: CCC 512–521, 531–534

Reflect on the **Faith**

- God is always working with us, cooperating with us, calling us closer to him. In some ways, this is what Advent is.
- During the season of Advent, we celebrate Jesus' original coming at the first Christmas, prepare for his second coming at the end of time, and live out his moment-to-moment coming into our lives now—in prayer and the sacraments, especially the Eucharist.
- We can prepare by saying, like John, "He must increase, but I must decrease" (John 3:30; see CCC 524). We ask the Lord to reign and be glorified in our lives.
- "Only when Christ is formed in us will the mystery of Christmas be fulfilled in us" (CCC 526). When Jesus is formed in us, we become more deeply and fully conformed to the mystery of his divinity within us.
- Becoming a child in relation to God is the condition for entering the kingdom.
- We are called to become children of God, in Baptism, born of above. Our Creator has become one of us, born of the Virgin.

Take It to **Prayer**

Father in heaven, we give you praise, and we give you glory. We give you a thanksgiving. Just like the angels sang your praises, singing, "Holy, holy, holy," saying, "Glory to God in the highest," the angels continue to sing, "Hosanna." The angels continue to cry out your name in prayer, in praise, in thanksgiving, giving you glory. We too join our voices to the voice of the angels, singing, "Glory to God in the highest and on earth, peace to people of goodwill." We cry out like the angels in heaven singing, "Holy, holy, holy." We cry out, and we just praise you, Father. Help us to become like children in relation to you. Help us, help us to accept you and to let you love us. This is the love that can change our lives. It is the only love that can change the world. In Jesus' name, we pray. Amen.

Dive **Deeper**

Praise God for his glory made manifest in the poverty of the Holy Family and humility of the Christmas mystery. Ask God for an increase in the gift of humility by desiring to become like a child to gain admittance into the kingdom of heaven.

Reflect on the **Faith**

- Whenever we are contemplating mysteries, we ask the Lord for his grace, his guidance, and his illumination.
- Jesus' circumcision is a sign of Baptism. A Jewish male, in order to be brought into the covenant, had to be circumcised. What brings us into the New Covenant is Baptism. (See CCC 527.)
- We see the radical obedience of Mary and Joseph who brought the child Jesus to be circumcised.
- The Epiphany is a sign that salvation is for the whole world.
- As a Jew, Jesus was obedient to the Law of Moses. He did not create a new religion but fulfilled the Old Covenant, the religion that God had revealed and given to the people of Israel.
- Jesus was not "off mission" when he lived thirty years in a "hidden life"—that is, before he began his public ministry. He was totally consecrated to the mission that flowed from his divine sonship.
- God has a mission for our lives, too, and we are called to be consecrated to it. Our mission flows from our relationship with God and identity as his sons and daughters through Baptism.

Take It to **Prayer**

Father in heaven, we do trust you, and we know that we need you. We know that we need your light to guide us, your voice to call us by name. And so as we reflect on this, this infancy, the infancy mysteries, infancy narrative of Jesus, as we reflect on his being presented in the Temple, his being lost and being found, as we reflect on his hidden life in Nazareth and the silence that marked the vast majority of his life, the obedience that marked all of his life and the work that marked his life, we just ask you to enter into the silence of our own hearts. Enter into the ways in which you are calling us to be obedient not only to you but also to those people who are in our lives that you are calling us to be obedient to. Enter into our work, Lord God, with your grace. With your own hands you worked. So we ask that you, please, enter into the work of our hands. You have sanctified work. Help our work this day be sanctified in you. No matter what, what it is that we are doing, let it be all for your glory and for the salvation of the whole world. In Jesus' name, we pray. Amen.

Dive **Deeper**

JESUS TEACHING IN HIS FATHER'S HOUSE

We know very little about Jesus' early years. It is for this reason that sometimes we speak of his "hidden life." Here we see Jesus in the Temple among the teachers. Even from the young age of twelve, Jesus exhibited profound wisdom and understanding (see CCC 534).

Reflect on the **Faith**

- Jesus allows himself to vanquish the Tempter for us by entering into our weakness. He has been tested in the same way that we are, yet never sinned (see Hebrews 4:15).

Solitude, angels minister to him

- When John the Baptist saw Jesus walking along the Jordan River at the time of his baptism, he said to the disciples, "Behold, the Lamb of God, who takes away the sin of the world" (John 1:29; see CCC 536). Jesus is that lamb of sacrifice taking away the sins of the world. Recognition
- Christ's obedience is the heart of his sacrifice and the heart of redemption. He submits himself entirely to his Father's will out of love for the Father and love for us (see CCC 539).
- After Jesus is baptized, he goes into the wilderness for forty days, where he is tempted by the Evil One, yet does not sin (see CCC 538).
- If we know what the Father is asking us to do and do not do it, we are lost. But if we do it, we are saints—and we participate in the world's redemption.
- Each Lent, we as a Church recognize the forty-day mystery of Jesus in the desert (see CCC 540).

40 days in the temptation to take the easier way. He did not. Jesus entered into our weakness

Take It to **Prayer**

Father in heaven, you know us. You know our name. You know our weaknesses. You know our great need for you. And we ask that you, please, meet us in our self-abasement, meet us in our weakness. We ask you to, please, meet us in our hesitancy and in our littleness. Meet us in our trials. When we find ourselves, Lord God, in the wilderness, when we find ourselves in a place of temptation, and even when we find ourselves in a place where we have failed the temptation and we have said no to you and yes to the tempter, help us even then, Lord God. Help us even then to know that we can count on you, to know that we can trust you. Help us to trust you in our brokenness. Help us to trust you in our wilderness and in our weakness. Meet us there, find us there, and bring us to your heart. In Jesus' name, we pray. Amen.

Dive **Deeper**

Was the baptism of John based on a Jewish ritual?

Much of Catholic tradition has deep roots in Judaism—which makes sense, because the Jews were entrusted with God's revelation as his Chosen People, and Jesus, as the Messiah, was the fulfillment of the Old Covenant. The sacrament of Baptism is prefigured in such Old Testament events as the Flood, and the passage of the Israelites through the Red Sea.

In Jewish tradition, baptism was meant for converts, as a symbol of "washing away" one's former self and becoming new as part of the people of Israel. Water's ability to cleanse was also significant for the Jews because of their strict purity laws and rituals. The baptism offered by John the Baptist, while not the sacramental Baptism that we receive as Christians, was more than an initiation ritual, however. Along with his preaching about the kingdom of God being at hand, John used baptism as a means of urging people to turn away from their sins, inviting them to be purified of their old way of living and to prepare for the coming of the Messiah.

Further Reading: Joseph Cardinal Ratzinger, *Jesus of Nazareth*, chapter 1; "Baptism," Kaufmann Kohler, Samuel Krauss, *Jewish Encyclopedia*

Reflect on the **Faith**

- The job of a king was to do battle for his people. At his baptism, Jesus was anointed priest, prophet, and king, then went into the wilderness to battle the Evil One.
- In the Old Covenant, God established a kingdom and promised a kingdom. Jesus would bring back together the lost tribes of the house of Israel, to establish a kingdom that would never end.
- The kingdom of God is the Church on earth. When Jesus says, "Repent, for the kingdom of heaven is at hand" (Matthew 3:2), he is saying that he is establishing a Church now. (See CCC 541).
- When we have a relationship with the King through the sacrament of Baptism, we are brought into the kingdom by being initiated into the Church.
- We cannot live without the Church. We cannot come to know Christ without his Church.
- The kingdom in heaven is the Church triumphant. On earth, it is the Church militant. In purgatory, it is the Church suffering. Christ stands at the heart of the kingdom, his Church.
- Jesus also calls sinners to the table. Ultimately, there will have to be a change of heart and life. Everyone is called to the joy, but God "also asks for a radical choice: to gain the kingdom, one must give everything" (CCC 526).

Take It to **Prayer**

Father in heaven, we praise you, and we thank you. We thank you for sending your Son not only to save us from our sins but also to establish the kingdom, to make it possible that we could be part of your family, that we could be part of your Church, because in our baptism, Lord, you have brought us into the kingdom. In our baptism, you have not only made us new creations, made us your sons and daughters, but you have made us a people—people that transcend definitions and boundaries of race or ethnicity, of culture, of nationality, a people united in your Son, a people united in your Holy Spirit, and a people united because you are God our Father. We get to be part of your family. We get to be part of your Church. We get to be part of your kingdom on earth and ultimately your kingdom in heaven. Thank you. Receive our praise and receive our thanks this day, in Jesus' name. Amen.

Dive **Deeper**

The Church has been given authority from God to teach throughout all nations. Do you struggle with the word "authority"? Are there any teachings of the Church you currently wrestle with? Take some time today to ask for God's grace to know him better in his Church, the kingdom of God on earth.

Reflect on the **Faith**

- Jesus demonstrated that he was the Messiah through his miracles. These pointed to the fact that the kingdom of God is at hand and that he is the Anointed One, the Messiah, the king of the eternal kingdom (see CCC 537).
- Christ did not come to earth to preach, perform miracles, suffer, die, rise from the dead, ascend into heaven, and send us the Holy Spirit "to satisfy ... curiosity." He did those things so we could put our faith in him and trust in him (see CCC 548).
- He came to save us from the slavery of sin so that we can live as God's sons and daughters in the power of the Holy Spirit (see CCC 549).
- Jesus established a kingdom, of which he is the King. He gave the Church a structure, with a pope and the bishops, who teach with the authority of Christ.
- The Church is not just invisible; it does not just exist in our hearts. The Church exists tangibly among us today.
- The keys of the kingdom belong to Jesus; this is his kingdom. But he entrusted them to Peter, and they have been entrusted to every Pope since Peter, all the way down to the Holy Father right now. This is an amazing gift.

Take It to **Prayer**

Father in heaven, we know you are with us. We know that you love us. We know that we can trust in you. And we have confidence in you. We know that Jesus Christ, your Son, our Lord—that he demonstrated not only his messianic power, his messianic identity, through his signs and wonders; he also demonstrated his great care for us. He also demonstrated his great love for us through these miracles, through these signs and wonders, through these exorcisms because he wants everything that is dead in us to come to life, all those things that are good in us to be made whole. All those things that are holding us back and are keeping us from you, Father, he wants those things to be shed, to be gotten rid of that we be delivered from the power of the Enemy and brought into your kingdom, into your family even more fully than we are right now. Lord, whatever things attach to us, whatever things are clinging to us, whatever things we are clinging to right now that are holding us back from living freely in your kingdom, we ask you to help us to let them go. Help us by removing them from our lives according to your will, according to your will in all things, Father. In Jesus' name, we pray. Amen.

Dive **Deeper**

JESUS HEALS THE SICK

Jesus performed many "signs" or miracles that testified to the advent of the messianic age (CCC 547–549). Here we see Christ healing the sick at the pool of Bethesda.

Reflect on the **Faith**

- The transfiguration of Jesus is a foretaste of the kingdom. His ascent into Jerusalem is to fulfill the role of the king. Everything he does is to establish the kingdom and redeem us (see CCC 554).

- The glory that we will behold him with for eternity is the glory that he always has. As Jesus gives a glimpse of his glory, he teaches too that he must be crucified (see CCC 555).

- Jesus tells Peter he must work and suffer and die, for that is where Jesus is going (see CCC 556).

- Everything in Jesus' life is this mystery because it keeps revealing to us his identity and mission—and our identity and mission. Jesus is transfigured, and that is our destiny.

- As Jesus descends the mountain and enters into agony, brokenness, and suffering, he shares our path. He walked it before us, but he walks it with us now by giving us his Holy Spirit so that we are never alone.

Take It to **Prayer**

Father in heaven, we thank you. We thank you and just stand, stand in awe of you. We stand in awe of your Son. We stand in awe of how you reveal yourself to be, that you reveal yourself to be, the God who is the King of the universe, and at the same time, you are the God who enters into the worst we have to offer. You are the God who enters into the lowest places. Lord God, you entered into the lowest places in our lives. Yes, you are the God of glory, but you also don't hide from our shame. You are the God of power, but you are not afraid of our weakness. Be with us now in our shame. Be with us now in our weakness. Be with us now and forever. In Jesus' name, we pray. Amen.

Dive **Deeper**

THE TRANSFIGURATION OF CHRIST

Here we see the transfiguration of Christ. He is with Moses and Elijah, since Jesus fulfills both the Law and the Prophets. Below are Peter, James, and John, awestruck by Jesus' divine radiance (see CCC 554–556).

Reflect on the **Faith**

- There is much we do not know about Jesus' hidden life in Nazareth, but even his silence reveals something to us. It teaches us about obedience and the goodness of family and work (see CCC 553, 561, 564).
- We enter into the mysteries of Jesus—his miracles, gestures, prayer, and love for people—and meditate on them until we have conformed ourselves fully to him. It is the work of a lifetime (see CCC 562).
- In his book *Salvation: What Every Catholic Should Know*, Dr. Michael Barber says that salvation is not merely being saved from hell, although it is that. But salvation is being saved from being un-Christlike. We are saved so that we can conform ourselves to the Lord. We do this through the grace of the sacraments.
- One of the traditions in the Church has been to meditate on the mysteries of Jesus' life through praying the Rosary.
- We cannot come to Jesus unless we are willing to humble ourselves (see CCC 563).
- Most people are called to the vocation of marriage and family, so often it is through it that God wills to make us saints. Jesus' family life of work and obedience in Nazareth is our model. (See CCC 564.)
- Jesus knew that he would die for sinners, and he did this by choice (see CCC 569). All of Christ's life is lived out in free and humble obedience.
- All of Christ's life continues to teach us. One way for us to reflect on his life is by reading the Gospels. There his words, works, gestures, and love for people shine through the pages.

Take It to **Prayer**

Father in heaven, we give you thanks. We praise you so much. And we thank you. Let our lives be marked by gratitude, our lives be marked by thankfulness. As we enter into your mysteries, as we reflect on your mysteries, Lord, let us not just know what the mysteries are, let us not just know something about the details of your life, but help us to walk in those mysteries, help us to live and breathe in the midst of those mysteries, help us to be conformed to you in those mysteries. As you are obedient, as you love those who are lovable and you love those who are unlovable, help us to be obedient. Help us to love those who are lovable and love those who are hard to love because you love us even when we are unlovable. Help us to have that same love for others that you have for us. In Jesus' name, we pray. Amen.

Dive **Deeper**

Spend time with Jesus in Adoration today and humbly meditate on the mysteries of Christ's life to align yourself fully to him. Ask God to help you become a reflection of Christ's obedience and love to others around you in your own life.

Reflect on the **Faith**

- Every part of Jesus' life reveals the mystery of his life and teaching and is part of the redemptive work of God. But the preeminent work of redemption occurs in the paschal mystery of Christ—in his passion, death, and resurrection.
- The entire Old Testament is the story of how God lovingly and faithfully chose the Jewish people as his own, as his firstborn, and how he entered into a covenant with them in a powerful way.
- The early Christians saw Jesus as the fulfillment of everything they had been praying, hoping, and waiting for. They did not see his ministry as establishing a new religion.
- Jesus says that not a speck of God's law, essentially, will be done away with, and he also says that some had rejected the teaching of the Lord for the traditions of men (see Matthew 5:18 and 15:6). Jesus upheld God's law according to the truth, because he is Truth.
- Jesus recognized, of course, that God's presence dwelled in the Temple in a unique way—and he also taught that he was greater than the Temple.
- Jesus is fully man and fully God.
- Without the Jewish people, we would not have Jesus, who is the fulfillment of everything in the Old Testament.

Take It to **Prayer**

Father in heaven, we give you praise and glory. Thank you so much for the gift of your Son. Thank you so much for the Jewish people. We praise you and glorify you. We thank you for giving us the Hebrew Scriptures like the Old Testament. Thank you for calling us into relationship with your Son Jesus Christ, through Baptism, and giving us your Holy Spirit, and making us into your sons and daughters. Father, send your Holy Spirit right now so that we can hear your wisdom, hear the truth, and say yes to it with all of our hearts. In Jesus' name, we pray. Amen.

Dive **Deeper**

THE CRUCIFIXION OF CHRIST

The paschal mystery is the saving mystery of Christ's suffering, death, and resurrection (see CCC 571). Here we have a fifteenth-century depiction of Jesus' crucifixion.

Reflect on the **Faith**

- There were people—such as some of the elders, chief priests, and Sadducees—who conspired with the Romans to put Jesus to death, though his relationship with the people of Israel was one of love.

- Christ placed himself as the Author of the Law. Many in authority did not accept him for who he was, even though his mighty works validated and verified his authority.

- Jesus has the authority to give the definitive interpretation of the Old Covenant, of the Old Law, for he is its Author.

- Jesus did not come to abolish the Law but to fulfill it (see Matthew 5:17). At the same time, certain laws no longer apply because God's covenant is a living covenant. Jesus ultimately gives the Law its true interpretation and fulfillment in himself (see CCC 577–578).

- The moral laws are absolute. They are true and binding at all times in all places for all people.

- Certain laws are no longer applicable because the context for which they were enacted no longer exists.

- Laws governing worship in the Temple ended because the Temple itself ceased to exist. Laws for the governance of the people of Israel ended because the kingdom of Israel—as it existed in the Old Covenant—ceased to exist.

- Jesus tells us the moral law must reach not only our actions but also our hearts. This moral law is still in effect.

Take It to **Prayer**

Father in heaven, we give you praise and glory. We thank you for, we thank you for the Law, we thank you for the gift of the Jewish dietary laws, we thank you for the gift of the Jewish Temple laws, we thank you for the gift of the eternal laws that you have revealed to us, those moral laws that are true at all times in all places for all people. Lord God, we also give you thanks that in you, you have offered the definitive interpretation of many of these laws. You have revealed to us who it is you are and how it is you want us to come to know you, how it is you want us to worship you and to love you as best we possibly can with your grace. Send us your grace right now so that we can know you and love you and worship you the way you've asked but also the way you deserve. On our own, we can never do this. So please send your grace upon us this day and every day. In the name of Jesus, we pray. Amen.

Dive **Deeper**

How do we know which laws in the Old Testament are still binding on us, as Christians, and which are not?

This is an important question. The *Catechism* explains how the laws from the Old Testament have been fulfilled in Christ and his Church—that is, in the life, prayer, and sacramental worship of the Christian community. In each part of the *Catechism*, we are shown how we as Christians are to live according to the new law of Christ, sharing in the life of Christ, who is priest, prophet, and King.

The new law, as Jesus makes clear, is not an abolition of the Law and the Prophets but their fulfillment (see Matthew 5:17; CCC 577) because *he* is the fulfillment of the Old Covenant. The *Catechism* therefore says that the Jewish laws had a "pedagogical meaning"—that is, they were intended to point beyond themselves, teaching something—and that Jesus is himself the "divine interpretation" of what that meaning is (see CCC 582). In the Old Covenant, the Temple and kingdom laws protected the revelation that God gave to his people before the coming of Christ. They specified how God was to be understood and worshipped by a people separated from the idolatry of the surrounding nations. This revelation was fulfilled and made flesh in Jesus, who opened this truth to all peoples, uncovering the universal meaning of the specific laws. In the fullness of revelation in Christ, every detail of the law found its fulfillment and meaning. These laws are now universalized and interiorized, teaching perennial spiritual principles. Those that seemed to teach separation between peoples point to separation from sin and error, setting free every person for worship of the one true God.

Key reading: CCC 577–582

Reflect on the **Faith**

- The Temple was the primary place of worship of God for the Israelites; it was the only place where one could offer a sacrifice to the Lord. The whole life of a Jewish person would be connected in some way to the Temple.
- Just as Jesus was the fulfillment of the Law, he was also the fulfillment of the Temple.
- The Temple was critically important in Jesus' life (see CCC 583–584).
- God made the world and human beings and revealed himself so we could share in his divine life in a relationship with him.
- When we worship God in the place of his presence, we are drawn further into a relationship of obedience, love, and trust with him.
- Jesus instituted a new and eternal kind of worship (see CCC 585).
- The night before Jesus died, he gave us the new and eternal covenant at the Last Supper, saying: "Take, eat; this is my body ... Drink of it, all of you; for this is my blood of the covenant, which is poured out for many for the forgiveness of sins" (Matthew 26:26–28). "Do this in remembrance of me" (Luke 22:19). (See also Luke 22:20 and Mark 14:22–24.)

Take It to **Prayer**

Father in heaven, we give you praise; we give you glory. We thank you for this moment. We thank you, above all, for your Son, Jesus. We thank you for the Holy Spirit that you have poured into our hearts as baptized Christians. We thank you for the gift of worship. We thank you that in your Son, you have fulfilled all worship of old, and you have placed in our hands and our lives the new and eternal covenant, the new and eternal way you want us to worship you, which we see in sign and in shadow now but, ultimately, we will see and be able to do face-to-face in your presence for all eternity. Lord God, open our minds and our hearts to understand and love your Temple. Open our minds and our hearts to understand and love how the Temple is fulfilled in your Son, Jesus Christ. In Jesus' name, we pray. Amen.

Dive **Deeper**

Every relationship takes time to build trust. Do you trust that God is with you always? Spend time in prayer asking God to open your heart to his presence to be drawn deeper into a relationship of obedience, love, and trust with him today.

Reflect on the **Faith**

- The people of Israel were formed over centuries to know the one true God. They heard his voice, spoken through the prophets and the words of Scripture in the Old Testament.
- Jesus then appeared and invited his people to faith in him in the same way and to the same degree that the Lord had invited faith and belief in himself in the Old Covenant. This caused scandal.
- C. S. Lewis in his book *Mere Christianity* explains that Jesus did not just claim to be a prophet or a holy person; he claimed to be God. There are only three explanations: either he was a liar, he was disconnected from reality (a lunatic), or he was truly who he said he was—the Lord.
- In asking the people to accept him as the Author of salvation and the Author of the universe, Jesus was asking them for an amazing amount of faith.
- Jesus demonstrates and proves that he is who he says he is—God himself. His signs and wonders point to the fact that he is God. He forgives sins and heals people. Ultimately, we see that he is God in the resurrection. (See CCC 594.)
- We need to ask God, by his grace, to come and meet us in our ignorance and hardness of heart so that we can truly accept and love him.

Take It to **Prayer**

Father in heaven, we give you praise and glory. Thank you for your Son. Thank you for revealing his deepest identity to us as that second Person of the Trinity. Thank you for revealing your Son to us as God himself incarnate in the flesh. Thank you for giving your Son to us and revealing that his mission par excellence was not only to fulfill the Law, not only to fulfill the Temple, but to redeem all humanity. Thank you so much. Thank you for the gift of faith. Help us when we struggle with our faith. Help us to say yes to you. When we struggle with our faith, help us to submit ourselves to you in humble obedience and humble trust, this day and every day. In Jesus' name, we pray. Amen.

Dive **Deeper**

What did most Jews at the time of Jesus think the Messiah would be like?

The Jews of Jesus' time had different views on how the kingdom of God would come about and what the Messiah would be like. They knew that what the prophet Isaiah had preached of the exiles returning to a restored land, a new kingdom of Israel, had yet to be fulfilled. Many of Jesus' contemporaries expected a political Messiah who would bring about this kingdom by overthrowing foreign oppressors by military means.

Jesus' reluctance to be proclaimed Messiah during his public ministry can be understood in the light of these expectations, expectations that were raised by his many miracles and healings, as well as by his confrontations with authority figures (see John 4:25–26; 6:15; Matthew 22:41–46). The Gospels vividly present the disciples struggling to understand the surprising nature of Jesus' messiahship. For example, we see Peter rightly identifying Jesus as the Messiah, only to be severely rebuked for not appreciating his redemptive mission as the Suffering Servant (see Matthew 16:16–23). But, as the *Catechism* teaches, there was a "small Remnant, the people of the poor," who were able to recognize in Jesus the authentic coming of Israel's redemption (see CCC 711).

The *Catechism* explains that Jesus faced the religious authorities with a completely "surprising" fulfillment of God's promises, a fulfillment that helps us to "understand the Sanhedrin's tragic misunderstanding of Jesus" (CCC 591). The incarnation is a "unique and altogether singular event" (CCC 464). In sending his only begotten Son, God the Father "acted far beyond all expectation" (CCC 422). God's goodness and grace were infinitely more than expected.

Key reading: CCC 436–440, 587–594, 711–714

Reflect on the **Faith**

- As the *Catechism* tells us, all "sinners were the authors" of Christ's Passion (CCC 598). It was our sin that killed our Lord Jesus Christ. And we have to take responsibility for that.
- We pray for reconciliation for all to take place in our day and age—that we and the Jewish people come to know Jesus Christ fully.
- In the book of Genesis, we read the story of Joseph and his brothers, who sell him into slavery. God brings Joseph to a position of authority, and he helps to spare people from famine. In the end, Joseph acknowledges that what his brothers meant for evil, God used for good (see Genesis 37–50).
- God can take even the worst brokenness and bring about great good. As Christians, we believe this is what happened with Jesus' death and resurrection. Our sins crucified Jesus, but God used his death to bring about the greatest thing that has ever happened—our salvation and our redemption.
- St. Francis of Assisi said, "It is you who have crucified him and crucify him still, when you delight in your vices and sins" (quoted in CCC 598).
- We must never try to evade blame. We must always take responsibility for our part in Christ's suffering and death.

Take It to **Prayer**

Father in heaven, we give you praise, and we give you glory. We thank you for giving us your Son. We thank you that in the midst of our brokenness, your Son, Jesus Christ, loves us. He loves us and he gives himself up for us. That he loved us, and he gave himself up for every one of us. There's not one person on this planet who has ever lived, is living, or will live for whom you did not die, for whom you did not rise from the dead. So we ask you to change our hearts, to heal our hearts. But also to heal the brokenness and whatever kind of division there is between the Christian people and the Jewish people, heal whatever kind of division there is between the people of the covenant and the people of the New Covenant. Lord God, you love us. We also ask that you, please, help all of us to deep and full conversion. Those of us who profess faith in Jesus, we ask you to, please, knit our hearts together and help us to be fully belonging to you. And also, the Jewish people with whom you established your covenant, we ask that you bring them to a knowledge of you as well because there is no one, there is no one whom you did not die for. There is no one whom you do not live for. There is no one to whom you do not extend your grace, so help us all to say yes to your grace this day and every day. In Jesus' name, we pray. Amen.

Dive **Deeper**

THE TRIAL OF CHRIST

Pictured here is Christ before the high priest (see CCC 596). We deny Christ and hold him up to contempt through our sins and vices (see CCC 598).

Reflect on the **Faith**

- Christ died for our sins.
- Though God knows all things, we still get to be free in our lives.
- God, who is sinless and blameless, had such love for us that even though he never sinned, he took upon himself our sins.
- In the Old Testament, one kind of offering was a sacrifice of atonement, or sin offering. Jesus became that sin offering for us.
- Why did he do this? He did it because he loves us. This is God's initiative. (See CCC 604–605.)
- Jesus died for all people, without exception. The Council of Quiercy in the year 853 stated: "There is not, never has been, and never will be a single human being for whom Christ did not suffer" (CCC 605).
- Those words should be embedded deeply into our hearts. When we are talking with anybody or looking in the mirror, we should recognize this is true.
- This is why we pray for those who do not yet know Christ. God has so much life and love and joy that he wants for the entire world.
- There is so much in our hearts that tempts us to disqualify ourselves. Let us pray for each other that we not only can believe with our minds that Jesus died for each person, but that we can take that truth deep into our hearts and live it today and every day.

Take It to **Prayer**

Father in heaven, you have loved us. You gave yourself up for us in your Son, Jesus Christ. You sent us your Holy Spirit. Help us to say yes to you. Lord God, we know that our sins have created a gap between you and us. We know that your love bridges that gap. We know that there was a point in time, in the fullness of time, when you sent your own Son, born of woman, born under the law, to save us. Extend that grace. Extend that salvation once again to us today. Help us to confidently call upon you, to call upon the name of your Son, Jesus Christ, to call upon your Holy Spirit that we might have new life and freedom in you, this day and every day. We make this prayer in Jesus' name. Amen.

Dive **Deeper**

Jesus fulfilled his obedient "yes" to the Father on the cross. Life can be difficult and filled with many hardships, but Jesus is with you through all the hardest moments of your life. Take fifteen minutes today to pray in front of a crucifix and invite Our Lord into your sufferings.

Reflect on the **Faith**

- Even the Incarnation is a "yes" of Jesus' obedient love to his Father. Every breath he took was an offering to the Father in love. (See CCC 606.)
- Jesus came to save us (see CCC 608). He loved his Father, and he loved us, no matter what it cost.
- Jesus is the Paschal Lamb. Lambs were offered as sacrifice as a foreshadowing of the atonement. Jesus is the true "Lamb of God, who takes away the sin of the world" (John 1:29; see CCC 608).
- Jesus makes this sacrifice freely, and the sign of that free gift is the Eucharist (see CCC 610–611).
- We can experience this every day by going to Mass—we are able to be participants in what Jesus himself has done.
- This *Catechism in a Year* is about conversion so that our hearts have more space to love God because of his grace and because we are getting to know who he is in a deeper way. And so if we have the opportunity to go to Mass today, let's take that step because we get to be part of the offering of Jesus to his Father.

Take It to **Prayer**

Father in heaven, give us insight into the heart of your Son, Jesus Christ. Give us insight into your heart. Give us insight into your will and how it unfolds in the middle of this broken and the middle of this beautiful world. Lord God, in our sufferings, help us to have the trust that Jesus had. Lord God, in our confusion, help us to have the love that Jesus had. Lord, in our lives, help us to have that same offering, that same willingness to offer everything in our lives to you as Jesus offered everything, his whole life, as an offering to you. Help us to trust you and to love you, for you are love. In Jesus' name, we pray. Amen.

Dive **Deeper**

JESUS IN HIS AGONY

Shown here is Jesus in the Garden of Gethsemane, contending with the horror of his impending suffering and death. He chooses to drink the chalice of suffering in obedience to the Father and for our sake (see CCC 607).

Reflect on the **Faith**

- Every priest offers up sacrifices, but Jesus is the priest who does not offer up a sacrifice outside of himself. He is the priest who *is* the sacrifice as well (see CCC 614–615).
- Out of love for us, Jesus offered us his sacrifice, unmerited on our part. And we are called to participate in it. Our lives are meant to be conformed to the "yes" of Jesus to his Father (see CCC 618).
- The Mass is the unbloody sacrifice of Jesus Christ, offered to the Father in the power of the Holy Spirit. Every time we celebrate and participate in the Mass, it gives glory to the Father and it redeems the world.
- Jesus is the one mediator between God and man. No human person could ever bear the sins of everyone, but he is a divine Person who has joined himself to humanity. (See CCC 616, 618.)
- We are invited to participate in the sacrifice that gives glory to the Father and that redeems the world.
- This is the Good News that we have this world that is good but fallen, and we are good but fallen, and into this world, good but broken, God's love has come. There is a God who cares about you, who knows your name, who loves you, and who even offered himself for you. That is amazing news.

Take It to **Prayer**

Father in heaven, we praise you. And we give you glory. We thank you so much for giving us your only Son whom you love to be a sacrifice for sinners. We thank you, Jesus Christ. We thank you for your obedience to the Father. We thank you for not only being the model of what it is to trust in the Father, but also for being the priest, for being the sacrifice, for being the one who not only offered but the one who was offered. Help us to say yes as well. Help us to have the same obedience that you had, Jesus, to the Father. And Father, may everything that we do this day—whether it be full of joy or full of pain, whether it be full of love or full of grief, we ask that everything we go through today be offered to you just like Jesus offered everything to you. It is in his name that we pray. Amen.

Dive **Deeper**

How was the death of Jesus a unique and definitive sacrifice?

The death of Jesus on the cross is the unique and definitive sacrifice because it is God's gift of himself for the redemption of the world—a gift *from* the Father *of* the eternal Son, offering himself up in the flesh he took on in the incarnation. As the *Catechism* tells us, "Jesus' violent death was not the result of chance in an unfortunate coincidence of circumstances, but is part of the mystery of God's plan" (CCC 599).

A vivid instance of the disciples' awakening to the reality of Jesus' sacrifice is the encounter on the road to Emmaus (see Luke 24:13–35). Jesus opened the eyes of these two disciples to see the reality of his death as a unique and definitive sacrifice. He taught them how the Scriptures spoke of him and of his sacrifice on the cross, speaking of the serpent raised up, the rejected and suffering servant, the blood of the lamb and death of the firstborn, the covenants and sacrifices, the offering of Isaac, the only son of Abraham. Our Lord showed them how the Scriptures pointed to this New Covenant. Then he celebrated this new covenant with them by breaking bread—and they finally recognized him and saw things as they are.

Key reading: CCC 599–623

Reflect on the **Faith**

- Because Jesus loves us so fully and united himself to us so fully, he not only entered into suffering, but actually entered into death. He "tasted death" and experienced "the separation of his soul from his body" (CCC 624).
- When Jesus died—which involves the separation of body and soul—he, the second Person of the Trinity, "necessarily continued to possess his human soul and body, separated from each other by death" (CCC 626).
- Jesus' resurrection on the third day fulfilled his claim that he would rise and also fulfilled the promise that he would not see corruption. It was held that bodily decay would begin on the fourth day after death (see CCC 627).
- On earth for three days, Jesus fulfills the story of Jonah in the belly of the whale for three days.
- In Baptism, being immersed in water three times is a sign of Christ's descent into the earth for three days. In the sacrament, the Christian dies to sin with Christ to live a new life.
- As Jesus descended into death, we who are baptized descend into his death too. We enter into his death and rise to new life with him.

Take It to **Prayer**

Jesus Christ, you are the Redeemer. You are the Savior of the world. You are the offering for sin. And you are the Lamb of God who takes away the sin of the world. To accomplish your Father's plan, you allowed death to overwhelm you. To accomplish the Father's plan, you entered into death. You descended to hell. To accomplish the Father's plan, you rose from the dead and ascended to heaven. To accomplish your Father's plan, you sent the Holy Spirit into our lives. Lord God, we thank you and praise you. We just give you every good gift because you are the giver of every good gift. We give you all praise. All glory belongs to you. All of our hearts belong to you. All of our love goes to you. Help us to love you the way you deserve. In your holy name, Jesus, Father, Son, Holy Spirit. Amen.

Dive **Deeper**

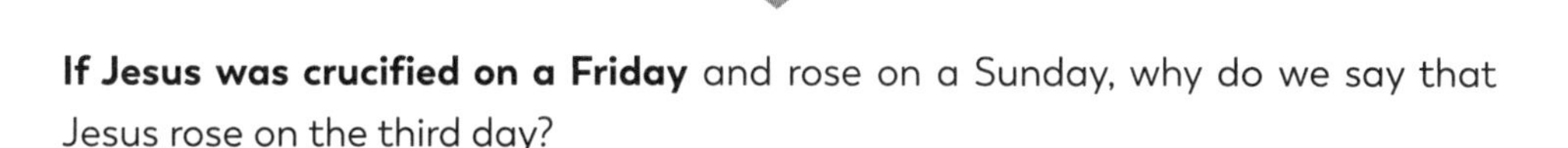

If Jesus was crucified on a Friday and rose on a Sunday, why do we say that Jesus rose on the third day?

The answer to this question turns on how we count a "day." In modern practice, we would not see Sunday as three full (i.e., twenty-four-hour) days after Friday. The ancient world, though, did not measure time in the same precise way we do. In the account of Jesus' death and resurrection, they would see Good Friday as the "first day," Holy Saturday as the "second day," and Easter Sunday as the "third day." So, indeed, it is appropriate for us to say that the resurrection of Jesus occurred after three days or "on the third day."

So Jesus did exactly as he promised—he was crucified and rose again after three days. How we count these days is less important than the truth that Jesus truly rose from the dead, not just spiritually but bodily. In doing so, Jesus redeemed this fallen world, opening up the life of grace and salvation to us—giving us the hope for one day being raised up, body and soul, to eternal life with him.

Further Reading: Pius X, *Lamentabili*, 36–37; Second Vatican Council, *Dei Verbum*, 19; Matthew 28:1; Mark 9:31; 16:1–2; Luke 24:1; John 20:1

Reflect on the **Faith**

- As the *Catechism* tells us, Jesus went to the abode of the dead "as Savior, proclaiming the Good News to the spirits imprisoned there" (CCC 632).
- In Scripture, *Sheol* is the Hebrew term for the "abode of the dead." Those there were "deprived of the vision of God ... while they await[ed] the redeemer" (CCC 633).
- When Christ came, he brought the souls of the righteous to heaven.
- This was different from eternal hell, which is permanent separation from God. "Jesus did not descend into hell to deliver the damned" (CCC 633). Those who have chosen against God cannot change their choice.
- For the righteous waiting for the Lord, the abode of the dead would be a place of peace and rest in the bosom of Abraham. For the damned, it would be the place of torment that hell actually is.
- Jesus' mission was for all men at all times and all places. Everyone saved—those who died before, during, or after the time of Jesus—shares in the redemption. (See CCC 634.)
- When Jesus descended to the realm of the dead, he went to rescue and deliver all of those who had chosen God before he opened the gates of heaven.
- In the Incarnation, the sacraments, his grace, and his Holy Spirit, God comes to us to deliver us.
- God did not create us to be prisoners in hell. We choose Jesus.

Take It to **Prayer**

Father in heaven, we give you praise. We thank you so much for bringing us to this moment. We thank you so much for the gift of your Son. We thank you so much for the fact that his love knows no bounds, that even the abode of the dead is not out of bounds for your love. We thank you for the fact that Christ descended into hell, that he descended to the abode of the dead to rescue the righteous. Help us to walk with righteousness. Help us to walk in right relationship with you so that we can live forever in right relationship with you. In Jesus' name, we pray. Amen.

Dive **Deeper**

In prayer today, spend time contemplating the Latin phrase *memento mori* in remembrance that you will die. Consider Christ's deliverance of the souls held captive in the abode of the dead and his great love desiring to rescue the righteous from death and grant the faithful eternal life.

Reflect on the **Faith**

- The resurrection of Jesus truly happened in history. Jesus did not merely rise "in the hearts of the believers" but literally rose bodily from the dead (see CCC 639).
- The empty tomb, as well as Jesus' appearances to Mary Magdalene and the other holy women, to Peter and the other apostles, and to more than five hundred people at once demonstrate the historical fact of the bodily resurrection of Jesus from the dead.
- This is a fundamental truth about Christianity. If Jesus has not risen from the dead, then our Faith is worthless (see 1 Corinthians 15:12–19).
- Not only did the apostles and others witness this, but they were transformed. They went from being discouraged and frightened to being bold and courageous because of the fact that they saw the risen Christ.
- No one would give his or her life for a lie. These men and women bore witness to the truth that they saw Christ risen from the dead—and it cost them everything.
- The Resurrection is a historical fact. It happened. Jesus Christ is Lord of the living and of the dead. He has conquered death, and he now lives for the glory of the Father.

Take It to **Prayer**

Father in heaven, we give you praise. Thank you so much for your Son's resurrection. Thank you so much, not only for the fact that he gave himself out of love, that he lived a life of obedience to redeem us and to glorify you, but also thank you for his resurrection. Thank you for the gift of proving to us that he is who he says he is in the resurrection from the dead. We thank you for inviting us to have a share in that resurrection. As you have invited us to participate in his passion, as you've invited us to participate in his suffering, you also, Lord God, you also invite us to participate in his resurrection. And so this day, we rejoice. Because this day we know that you are the conqueror of death. We know that you are the one who was slain and yet still live forever and ever. You are the Alpha and the Omega, the beginning and the end, the one who was, who is, and who is to come. And we praise and glorify you in Jesus' name. Amen.

Dive **Deeper**

How should we understand the resurrection of Jesus?

When the New Testament speaks of the resurrection of Jesus, it does not mean the mere resuscitation of his earthly corpse—that is, of Jesus simply bodily returning to this life. Scripture makes clear that, in the resurrection, Jesus entered into a new *kind* of life. We can see this in the disciples who encountered the resurrected Christ—Mary Magdalene did not even recognize him at first. Clearly, something about him had changed. When he appeared to the disciples, they were uncertain and confused. Was this a ghost? No, Jesus ate with them and later told Thomas to place his hands in his nail marks and side. Upon encountering the resurrected Jesus, his followers had to grapple with something they did not yet understand (see CCC 643–646).

In Jesus, God fulfills *all* his promises ... but not in *any* of the ways the people expected. This breaking of human expectations is one of the reasons that the disciples, as eyewitnesses to the resurrection, encountered a reality they did not expect and could not understand. But belief in the resurrected Jesus transformed them and invigorated their faith, prompting them to spread the Gospel throughout the world and suffer any pains, even death, in service of Christ.

Key reading: CCC 638–644, 992–996

Reflect on the **Faith**

- Jesus raised some people from the dead, but they were just brought back to normal human existence (see CCC 646).
- When Jesus rose, he had a different condition, "beyond time and space." The risen glorious body of Jesus is "filled with the power of the Holy Spirit" and will never die. (See CCC 646.)
- "The Father's power 'raised up' Christ his Son and by doing so perfectly introduced his Son's humanity, including his body, into the Trinity" (CCC 648).
- Christ emptied himself and took on human nature, but then he did not abandon it in his resurrection. Instead, he took humanity to himself. (See CCC 648.)
- The resurrection is brought about by the Holy Trinity. When one person of the Trinity is present and acts, they all are present and act. (See CCC 648.)
- Jesus truly died, and in rising from the dead, he truly is alive. He lives now and eternally.

Take It to **Prayer**

Father in heaven, we give you praise and glory. Thank you so much for bringing us to this moment. Thank you for bringing us to this day, day 92. We thank you for your grace. Thank you for the Spirit that you have given to us, the same Spirit that raised Christ from the dead, that dwells in us now. We ask that you help us to be cooperative, to be attentive, to be receptive to your Holy Spirit so that in all things we can do your will, Father. In Jesus' name, we pray. Amen.

Dive **Deeper**

The glory of the resurrection transcends time and space. Take five minutes today to encounter Christ's abounding love and appreciate his power assuming humanity into divinity through the gift of the resurrection.

Reflect on the **Faith**

- Reading the *Catechism* is not merely about transfer of information but about transformation.
- Today we are talking about what the resurrection has to do with us.
- If Jesus has not been raised from the dead, then what are we believing in? We would be believing in someone who had some nice things to say but ultimately died like any other human being, and that would be the end of the story.
- But the Resurrection is true. It means Jesus really is who he says he is, and so everything he says is true. (See CCC 651.)
- Filial adoption is a technical term that basically means that we are adopted as sons and daughters of God the Father. Because of the life, death, and resurrection of Jesus, we now are capable of having God as our Father and also Jesus as our brother. (See CCC 654.)
- Christ's resurrected body is like the foreshadowing of what we are called to experience. Right now, we experience the gifts of his grace, being his brethren, and being the Father's adopted sons and daughters.

Take It to **Prayer**

Father in heaven, we praise you and thank you. We give you glory today. We ask that you please receive our praise and thanks. Thank you so much for being love and for sending your Son to be one of us, to suffer and die for us, for our forgiveness of sins, but also in rising from the dead and conquering death to manifest the resurrection. You love us so much that you continue to give us your Holy Spirit of forgiveness, your Holy Spirit of redemption, your Holy Spirit that unites us to you and allows us to call you Father. Let that Spirit that raised Christ Jesus from the dead dwell in us. Help us to anticipate the glorified resurrected bodies that you desire us to experience for all eternity, and help us to say yes to you this day. Help us to say yes to your passion. Help us to say yes to your resurrection. Help us to participate in your suffering and cross, and help us to participate in your glory and resurrection. In Jesus' name, we pray. Amen.

Dive **Deeper**

Through the resurrection of Jesus, we are reinstated in grace and become adopted sons or daughters of God the Father. In prayer, thank the Father for what he has done and what he has yet to do in our lives out of love for his beloved children.

Reflect on the **Faith**

- In his ascension, Jesus unites humanity to divinity. The ascension completes his saving work.
- Humanity on its own cannot enter heaven. It is Jesus who unlocks the gates of heaven. He brought our humanity to heaven, so we now can come to the Father. (See CCC 661.)
- Jesus ascended to heaven, where he dwells as the eternal priest. He continually offers himself as a sacrifice of love to the Father.
- The innermost life of the Trinity is an eternal exchange of love. The Son, from all eternity, has been offering himself in love to the Father.
- With the ascension, there is a new reality introduced into the life of the Trinity where the Son of God, who has always been offering himself to the Father in love, is also offering humanity to the Father through his one eternal sacrifice on the cross.
- Whenever the holy sacrifice of the Mass is offered, the ministerial priest shares in the one eternal priesthood of Christ. Jesus himself is the principal actor of the Liturgy.
- When we participate in Mass, we are tapping into that once-for-all sacrifice—not only what happened on Calvary and at the Last Supper, but what is constantly, permanently happening in heaven.
- In summary, the ascension of Jesus: 1) completes the work of redemption; 2) unites humanity to divinity; 3) lets us come to the Father in heaven in a way that was impossible before; and 4) enables our participation in Mass on earth to be a participation in the worship that is happening in heaven.

Take It to **Prayer**

Father in heaven, we thank you. We thank you for the gift of your Son. We thank you for the gift of his life, his suffering, his death, his resurrection. And today, Lord, we thank you for the gift of the ascension of your Son, Jesus, into heaven. Thank you for bringing the humanity that you took upon yourself that you united to yourself. Thank you for bringing that humanity into heaven so that we could have access to you. And you permanently have access to us. Help us to always recognize that, as the Son continually offers himself to you, Father, that we are united to that offering, that we become part of that offering, participate in that offering, so that we ourselves may offer ourselves to you continually in this life and with your grace, in your presence, and in eternal life forever. In Jesus' name, we pray, in the name of the Father, and of the Son, and of the Holy Spirit. Amen.

Dive **Deeper**

THE ASCENSION OF CHRIST

Shown here is the ascension of Christ. He takes his place at the right hand of the Father and never ceases to make intercession for us. Jesus goes to prepare a place for us and beckons us to follow him to heaven (see CCC 666).

Reflect on the **Faith**

- Christ's kingdom has been established on earth through the Church. He reigns in the Church because he is exalted in heaven at the right hand of the Father.
- This kingdom of Christ on earth is still under attack today. We are called the Church militant, the Church that continues to fight in the name of Jesus Christ against the powers of evil.
- Though Jesus is with us, we await his return with power and great glory at the end of time.
- Jesus Christ is the fulfillment of every promise that God made to the people of Israel. He has not voided his covenant. Christianity is the fulfillment of Judaism. (See CCC 673–674.)
- Each of us needs to have a personal relationship with Jesus. Yet, as Christians, we are called not only to love our Head, Jesus, but also his Body, the Church.
- Jesus has won the definitive victory over sin, evil, and death, but there is still a battle to be fought on earth, for there are consequences to evil. Even the Church has been affected by this evil.
- We are called to worship God now in spirit and in truth and to give witness to him.
- This is a time of waiting and watching, of being vigilant and fighting. Part of that fight is simply bringing what is dark into the light.

Take It to **Prayer**

Father in heaven, we ask you, please send your Holy Spirit into our hearts that we can be fully converted to you. Please send your Holy Spirit into the hearts of all of our friends, our family members who have walked away from the Church, those who have never encountered you and your love. We ask you to send your Holy Spirit upon all people who share other beliefs that they may be drawn by your Spirit of truth to your very heart, which is truth. Lord God, your Son Jesus Christ declared that he is the Way, the Truth, and the Life. No one comes to you except through him, and so we ask, please help us all, all of us. Whether we are professing Christians or not, help us all to come to know the Way, the Truth, and the Life, Jesus Christ, and by that knowledge, and by that following of him, to come to you, Father. We make this prayer in the name of Jesus Christ, our Lord. Amen.

Dive **Deeper**

Sin makes us focus on ourselves and our own desires. Find a moment today in which you can selflessly serve someone in need and give witness to God's greatness.

Reflect on the **Faith**

- "Before Christ's second coming the Church must pass through a final trial that will shake the faith of many believers." There will be "persecution" and "religious deception." (See CCC 675.)

- There will be the deception of the Antichrist and a false messianism. People will believe that something can be done in the world without the Lord to solve their problems and to usher in a new time of peace, prosperity, and salvation. There is always a temptation to replace God with something else.

- As Christians, we recognize that progress can be made in this world, but no program, person, government, policy, or culture can ever usher in the messianic age.

- Even though the Lord God had chosen the people of Israel and revealed himself to them, they repeatedly turned away from him and attempted to replace him with something else.

- Humanity can be tempted to glorify itself—and put education, politics, good deeds, technology, science, or other people in place of God. While such things can be good, every time we replace God with them, we are turning away from him. This is idolatry.

- We should expect to follow our Lord in his death, in being misunderstood, rejected, hated, and killed.

- Mankind will face a universal judgment at the end of time, but each of us will face a judgment at the end of our lives. Our conduct on earth, no matter how hidden, will be brought to light.

- By being indifferent to God's love and "rejecting grace in this life"—such as ignoring the opportunity to go to confession—we judge ourselves (see CCC 679).

Take It to **Prayer**

Father in heaven, we trust in you, and we thank you. We praise your name, and we give you glory. We ask that you please reveal to our hearts your heart. Reveal the depth of your love for us to us, and help us to say yes to you. Help us to avoid the temptation toward idolatry. Help us to avoid the temptation towards the Antichrist. Help us to avoid the temptation to turn away from what you've given to us in favor of something new, in favor of something flashy, in favor of something that is not from you. Lord God, help us to strive with all of our hearts and our whole lives to help the people around us, but to never replace your kingdom with a pseudo, false kingdom. Help us to never replace you and your victory on the cross with any other kind of victory. Help us to live as you've called us to live. Help us to love as you have called us to love. Help us to be the hands and feet of Jesus Christ in this world by the power of your Holy Spirit. In Jesus' name, we pray. Amen.

Dive **Deeper**

CHRIST AT THE LAST JUDGMENT

Christ came first in humility and meekness, but at the end of time, he will come in glory and splendor to judge the living and the dead (see CCC 678). Michelangelo shows the justice at work in the Last Judgment.

Reflect on the **Faith**

- We have already talked about the very identity, the very nature of who the Holy Spirit is. Now we're going to talk about how the Holy Spirit interacts with us and what he does—how he is active in our salvation.

- St. Gregory of Nazianzus speaks of how God has revealed himself slowly over the course of time. God reveals himself as Father, then slowly reveals the Son, and then the Holy Spirit. (See CCC 684.)

- If we have come to know Jesus, it has always been by the power of the Holy Spirit.

- In the sacraments, it is the power of the presence of the Holy Spirit that takes what Jesus did and brings it to us right now in this present moment.

- We honor the saints and study their lives because when we look to them, we are seeing God's gifts on display. We are seeing what God can do in the life of an ordinary human being. That is what the Holy Spirit has done in the lives of the saints.

- Every time we pray as Christians, we pray in the power of the Holy Spirit, so let us pray for each other.

Take It to **Prayer**

Father in heaven, in the name of your Son, Jesus Christ, send your Holy Spirit into our hearts. Send your Holy Spirit to continue to sanctify us, to guide us, to help us trust in you, to help us have the supernatural gift of faith. Help us to have that supernatural gift of hope. Help us to have that supernatural gift of love that is driven, motivated, and strengthened by you. You are the Lord, the giver of life, who proceeds from the Father and the Son. Holy Spirit, come upon us now, and may the Father be glorified forever and ever. Amen.

Dive **Deeper**

How can we develop a relationship with the Holy Spirit?

Since he is infinite, God is the most profound mystery. It is impossible for us to understand him fully with our limited, human minds. Thankfully, he has given us ways to know him, most tangibly when the Son of God became man and lived among us. It is Jesus who shows us the Father (see John 14:8–11), and the example of his intimate relationship with his Father helps us to form a relationship with God the Father as well. But the imagery used in Scripture for the Holy Spirit—wind, breath, dove, fire—can feel somewhat abstract. Cultivating a relationship with the Holy Spirit requires more effort, a bit more "Catholic imagination." We can start by seeing in the Bible how the Spirit was active in Creation, in Jesus' ministry, and in the early Church. We might imagine the breath of the Spirit animating us, with his fire burning in our hearts, and picture ourselves in the upper room on Pentecost. What must that have been like? Finally, like any relationship, growing close to the Holy Spirit means spending intentional time with him, asking him to help us to know him. Pray to the Spirit, ask him to speak to your heart, and then listen.

Further Reading: Luke 1:35; John 14:15–17, 26–27; St. Basil the Great, "On the Holy Spirit"; Origen, *De Principiis*, "On the Holy Spirit," book 1, chapter 3; Pope Francis, "Morning Meditation in the Chapel of the Domus Sanctae Marthae," September 17, 2019

Reflect on the **Faith**

- When the Son and the Spirit act, they act together.
- A beautifully poetic way of describing this is that the Father is like the speaker, the Son is the Word, and the Spirit is the breath that accompanies the Word (see CCC 689).
- Father is spirit, and the Son is spirit; and the Father is holy, and the Son is holy; but "Holy Spirit" is the name of the third Person of the Holy Trinity.
- We are temples of the Holy Spirit.
- Every time we confess Christ's lordship, it is always by the power of the Holy Spirit.
- The Son is the advocate who comes to our aid; he is Emmanuel, who dwells among us. And the Holy Spirit also comes to our aid and advocates for us; he is the Paraclete, the Consoler, and the Spirit of Truth.

Take It to **Prayer**

Father in heaven, we give you praise and glory. We thank you for this opportunity to be here. Thank you for this incredible moment where we get to learn more about who you are. Holy Spirit, too often we forget about you. Too often you are the forgotten person of the Holy Trinity. We do not want to forget you. We forget you because we don't know. We forget you because of our lack of appreciation, our lack of memory, our lack of love. In this moment, help us to know more clearly so that we can love you, Holy Spirit. You are true God, from true God. Help us to love you. Help us to know you. Help us to walk in your power and your strength this day and every day. In Jesus' name, we pray. Amen.

Dive **Deeper**

God has given us the fruits of the Holy Spirit as sheer gifts. How are you using these gifts? Ask the Holy Spirit, the Consoler, to help you find ways to be patient, gentle, and kind to those who might be difficult to love today.

Reflect on the **Faith**

- Today we are going to look at symbols of the Holy Spirit. They are rooted in Scripture, but they also have a place today in the life of the Church.
- As human beings, it helps us to have symbols.
- Fire is an amazing image for the Holy Spirit. The Holy Spirit comes down upon the apostles and the disciples at Pentecost like "tongues as of fire" (Acts 2:3; see CCC 696).
- Every time a man is ordained a deacon, priest, or bishop, there is the laying on of hands. And that action goes all the way back to the apostles.
- Let us pray for the Holy Spirit to enter our hearts so that we can love God with all of our heart, mind, soul, and strength. We can only do this by the power of the Holy Spirit.

Take It to **Prayer**

Father in heaven, we give you praise and glory. Thank you so much for revealing yourself as Father. Thank you for giving us your Son as one of us and his humanity and divinity. And thank you for sending your Holy Spirit upon us. Thank you for your Holy Spirit's work in Creation, your Holy Spirit's work in redemption, the Holy Spirit's work of sanctifying this world. We ask that you please make us new, create us anew. Redeem us once again and save us for your sake so that we can glorify you and so that we can be instruments of your salvation in this world by the power of the Holy Spirit. In Jesus' name, we pray. Amen.

Dive **Deeper**

THE HOLY SPIRIT

Shown here is the famous window in St. Peter's Basilica. It portrays the Holy Spirit as a dove, as we see in Scripture (see CCC 701).

Reflect on the **Faith**

- Today we are going to talk about how God revealed himself in the Old Testament. We have these hints of the reality, the power, and the working of the Holy Spirit from the very beginning all the way to now.
- As Catholics, we talk about the Law, the Prophets, and the Wisdom Literature in the Bible, but we also say that all of it is prophetic because those people wrote under the inspiration of the Holy Spirit.
- After the Fall, man lost his likeness to God—that robe of sanctity, the holiness and righteousness that God had bestowed on Adam. We lost that, and the Son took on our human nature and "restore[d] it in the Father's 'likeness' by giving it again his Glory, the Spirit who is 'the giver of life'" (CCC 705) in Baptism.
- The Holy Spirit works in the midst of a place where there is no hope, and he gives hope.
- The Law was powerful in its ability to teach, but it could not give salvation. We need the Holy Spirit. (See CCC 708.)
- We are not called to be assimilated into the culture; we are called to live differently. That takes strength. That takes the Holy Spirit. Let us pray for each other that we can live this way, as Christians filled with God's Holy Spirit and led by him.

Take It to **Prayer**

Father in heaven, we praise you and we thank you. Thank you so much for bringing us to this moment. Thank you for bringing us to this day. Thank you for giving us the breath of life. And thank you for giving us this supernatural breath of life, your Holy Spirit, in our lungs, in our bodies, in our souls. Thank you for bringing us to new life. Thank you for restoring us to your likeness. Our God, we ask that you please send your Holy Spirit right now into the wounds of our minds—heal our memories; into the wounds of our hearts—heal our broken or calloused hearts. Send your Holy Spirit to us right now so that we can be your image and likeness in this world. In Jesus' name, we pray. Amen.

Dive **Deeper**

God remains faithful to his children and promises them the hope of redemption despite pain and suffering. Spend time in prayer reflecting how the Holy Spirit has worked through you this year, restoring your heart from a place to despair to one of hope and light.

Reflect on the **Faith**

- The Holy Spirit reveals through the prophets that the Messiah will come to the poor and exiled.
- In the Old Testament, the prophet Isaiah plays a significant part in preparing the people for the Messiah, and John the Baptist plays this role at the start of the New Testament, making way for Jesus Christ.
- Part of the promise of the kingdom of God is that one day every tear will be dried, and every wounded heart will be mended, but that day is not yet here.
- Only a short time after Jesus was conceived, John the Baptist recognized Jesus' divine presence from the womb and leapt for joy. It is impossible that a Christian could read this in Scripture and conclude that the child in the womb is not a person. This highlights the evil of abortion.
- It is miraculous how Jesus communicates through the Holy Spirit from the womb of the Blessed Virgin Mary to John the Baptist in the womb of Elizabeth.
- The Holy Spirit has not only been acting since Pentecost but also had been acting before that time through the prophets, especially through John the Baptist. The Holy Spirit has operated throughout all human history and is present to you now.

Take It to **Prayer**

Father in heaven, we ask you to please send your Holy Spirit upon us. In the name of Jesus, we ask you to send your Holy Spirit of truth, your Holy Spirit of prophecy, your Holy Spirit that speaks words of wisdom, and Holy Spirit that speaks words of conviction and consolation. Send that Holy Spirit, your Holy Spirit, into our hearts, into our minds, so that we can not only see how you have moved through the prophets and see how you moved in the life of John the Baptist, but so we can also see how you are continuing to move in our lives. Lord, let us never be deaf, let us never be numb to your voice and to your workings. Help us to always say yes to your will, this day and every day of our lives. In Jesus' name, we pray. Amen.

Dive **Deeper**

May we love God with abandon and imitate John the Baptist's leap for joy when encountering Jesus' divine presence. Ask the Holy Spirit to purify and enlighten your heart today in preparation to receive the Messiah.

Reflect on the **Faith**

- The *Catechism* highlights that everything Christ is doing is "a joint mission of the Son and the Holy Spirit" (CCC 727).
- We have talked about how the Holy Spirit revealed the Lord through the prophets, and now we are coming to this great moment when the Holy Spirit, in time, prepared the Blessed Virgin Mary and brought our Lord to the world (see CCC 722, 724).
- By the merits of her son's life, death, and resurrection, Mary was preserved from all stain of original sin.
- Sometimes people think that we are elevating Mary to a place that is beyond needing God. That is not true. It is the exact opposite: Mary was immaculately conceived by grace, by the complete gift of God (see CCC 722).
- Humility is "not thinking less of ourselves but thinking of ourselves *less*."[8] The humble person is always rejoicing and giving glory to God because they realize that everything they have comes from the Lord.
- Mary had the greatest capacity to receive God's gift. She was the "most humble" (CCC 722).
- Now Christ's mission—to reconcile us to God—is "the mission of the Church" (CCC 730). You and I are part of that mission.

Take It to **Prayer**

Father in heaven, in the name of your Son Jesus Christ, we ask you to please hear our prayer, receive our prayer, and send your Holy Spirit upon our lives, into our lives right now. Send your Holy Spirit to illuminate our minds that we can see clearly. Send your Holy Spirit to inflame our hearts so that we can love in truth and we can love in Spirit, that we can worship you in truth, that we can worship you in Spirit. We make this prayer in the mighty name of Jesus Christ, our Lord. Amen.

Dive **Deeper**

Take a few minutes to read Mary's canticle in Luke 1:46–55 and reflect on her beautiful prayer of thanksgiving to the Father, in the Holy Spirit, while carrying within her the Incarnate Son of God.

Reflect on the **Faith**

- God's love is effective. It does something. It forgives our sins.
- We recognize and praise God for the fact that through the Holy Spirit in the Church, the Lord has restored to us our right relationship with him.
- Jesus said, "You shall receive power when the Holy Spirit has come upon you; and you shall be my witnesses" (Acts 1:8). We have been given the power to bear witness to Jesus himself by the way we live and love—the way we treat people and forgive others.
- Pope Paul VI wrote in 1975 in *Evangelii Nuntiandi*, "Modern man listens more willingly to witnesses than to teachers, and if he does listen to teachers, it is because they are witnesses" (41). We have to not just say what we believe; we have to live what we believe in.
- We may know we are supposed to do what Jesus told us to do. But we are not just called to know it. We are called to live that fullness of life with the fruits of the Spirit.
- We have to pray because we can only live the fruits of the Spirit by the power given by the Holy Spirit. On our own, we cannot do this. But we are not on our own.

Take It to **Prayer**

Father in heaven, we love you, and we give you praise and thanks. Thank you so much for making us yours, for calling us to be your sons and daughters, and for giving us access to your heart, Father. Because you've given us, through Christ Jesus and in the Holy Spirit, access to your fatherly heart. So we thank you. Help us to approach you with confidence, approach you with humility, and approach you as you are. We make this prayer in the mighty name of Jesus Christ, our Lord. Amen.

Dive **Deeper**

What was the Old Testament feast of Pentecost? Is it related to our Christian feast of Pentecost?

The Jewish feast of Pentecost is one in a series of thanksgiving celebrations for the harvest. The word "Pentecost" comes from the Greek *pentekoste*, meaning "fiftieth." Thus, on the Jewish calendar, the feast of Pentecost was celebrated fifty days after Passover. The Jewish feast of Pentecost recognized the firstfruits of the harvest as God's faithful provision of all they needed, a celebration in thanksgiving for his loving care for them.

As an observant Jew, Jesus would have celebrated all the Jewish holy days, including Pentecost. After his passion, death, and resurrection, the feast of Pentecost takes on a new significance, while borrowing some of the symbolism of the Old Testament feast. For Christians, the feast of Pentecost (celebrated fifty days after Easter) retains some of the "harvest" connotations of the original feast by seeing Jesus to be the "first fruit" of God's ultimate gift—our salvation—by sending the Holy Spirit to sanctify us.

Further Reading: *Byzantine Catholics and the Feast of Pentecost*, Archeparchy of Pittsburgh; "Looking at the Jewish Roots of Pentecost," Fr. Dwight Longenecker, *Crux*, June 3, 2017; Leviticus 23:15–22

Reflect on the **Faith**

- The missions of Jesus Christ and the Holy Spirit are inseparable from each other and "brought to completion in the Church, which is the Body of Christ and the Temple of the Holy Spirit" (CCC 737).
- The mission of Christ and work of the Holy Spirit is made effective in the life of the Church.
- The Church, instituted by Jesus, communicates God's grace.
- The Holy Spirit continues to be the one who reveals Jesus to us.
- The Church is meant to teach and live the truth and to bring new life to others and bring others to this new life, just as Jesus did.
- Jesus did not just teach. Above all, he gave us access to the Father. Since that was his mission, it is our mission too.

Take It to **Prayer**

In Jesus' name, come Holy Spirit, and teach us how to pray. Father, in the name of your Son, Jesus Christ, send your Holy Spirit that we can learn how to pray, and we know how to live and have the strength to live as you're calling us to live, and we can know you more deeply and actually learn how to love even more your working and your Church and the Temple of the Holy Spirit that is tangible in this world. It isn't just spiritual but is visible in this world, in the Holy Catholic Church. We ask that you please open our eyes to be able to see that and open our hearts to receive this gift that you have given to us, because your Church, which is divine, is also human. And as human, it is broken. And as human, it is full of sinners like myself. So Father, in the name of your Son, Jesus, send your Holy Spirit, the soul of the Church, to us that we can receive your Body, we can serve your Body on earth, and that we can be a part of your mission to the world. Help us to be true witnesses of your life, death, and resurrection, true witnesses of your grace and mercy and power and love to this world. In Jesus' name, we pray. Amen.

Dive **Deeper**

Ask the Holy Spirit to teach you to pray. Sit in silence for a few minutes and ask the Holy Spirit to help guide you in your weakness to listen to the Lord's voice calling to you today.

Reflect on the **Faith**

- What we state about the Church has everything to do with what we have stated about the Father, Son, and Holy Spirit (see CCC 748–749).
- The Church is inseparable from the missions of Christ and the Holy Spirit. The starting point for understanding the Church is Christ Jesus (see CCC 748).
- Today, we will look at the four marks of the Church—one, holy, Catholic, and apostolic—as we declare in the Nicene Creed.
- Jesus promises to guide the Church into all truth, but we also recognize that, because of the brokenness of humanity, there is going to be darkness in our history. The brokenness does not come from God.
- The Church "belongs to the Lord," and the members of the Church belong to the Lord in a unique, powerful, very real way (see CCC 751).
- As members of the Body of Christ, it is worth meditating deeply on what we are part of.

Take It to **Prayer**

Father in heaven, in the name of your Son, Jesus Christ, we pray. We ask you to, please, no matter where we're at right now, send your Holy Spirit. Wherever we are right now, Lord, if we're at a place of discouragement, we ask you to please meet us in our discouragement. If we are in a place of confusion, we ask you to please meet us in that place of confusion. If we are in a place of joy, in a place of deep peace, please meet us, meet us in your joy, meet us in your peace. We know that we can trust you. We love you. And we dedicate our lives to you. Thank you for giving us the gift of your holy, Catholic, apostolic, and one Church. We thank you, and we praise your name. In Jesus' name. Amen.

Dive **Deeper**

Since you belong to the Lord by your baptism, ponder his plan for you as a member of the Body of Christ within the Church as you worship at Mass, participate in parish life, and recognize that you belong to the universal Church.

Reflect on the **Faith**

- Some amazing saints have lived up to the Church's teachings, while some terrible sinners have not.
- In the image of the sheepfold, we are Christ's flock, and he is the only gate through which we can enter—the only Savior. Christ said, "I am the good shepherd. The good shepherd lays down his life for the sheep" (John 10:11). (See CCC 754.)
- Jesus is the one savior. There is no salvation through any other name or person in the world.
- The symbol of the field is an image that Jesus fulfills when he says he is the true vine, and we are the branches. We can only bear fruit and have life if we are in Christ (see CCC 755).
- We can be justly upset with the failings of people in the Church.
- It is essential to remember that Christ loves the Church, and we are called to have hearts that love as he loves. We are called to have hearts that love Christ's Church.

Take It to **Prayer**

Father in heaven, you have called us. You are the teacher—your Son is the teacher. He is the great teacher. And you have given us, through your Son and the power of the Holy Spirit, the Church as our mother, our mother and our teacher. And so we just ask you to help us to have minds and hearts that are open to being taught, help us to have minds and hearts that are open to your Church in a way that maybe they haven't been open before. And we ask you to, please, give you permission, help us to give you permission to draw close to us in your Church, to teach us through your Church, and give us the willingness to trust you in your Church. We know we can't always trust the members of the Church. We cannot even trust ourselves, Lord God, but we do trust you. And you will never lead your Church astray. You will never abandon her, even in her brokenness. So give us hearts, give us minds that are open to being taught and hearts that are open to you and your Church. Give us this grace. Give us this Holy Spirit this day and every day. In the name of Jesus Christ, our Lord. Amen.

Dive **Deeper**

JESUS IS THE TREE OF LIFE

Scripture provides us with many symbols of the Church, of Christ's relationship to his people. One such image is portrayed here. Jesus is the vine, and we are the branches. He gives us life and vitality, whereas being cut off from him brings death (see CCC 755).

Reflect on the **Faith**

- The *Catechism* states that from the moment of the Fall, God planned for the Church (see CCC 758, 761). We were created with original justice in right relationship with God, but once sin was introduced and the relationship was severed, God wanted to repair it in his love.
- In the Old Testament, we see God revealing himself gradually and creating a unified people called to live in covenant with each other and the Lord simultaneously. This prefigures Christ's institution of the Church (see CCC 761).
- God wills the salvation of every person who ever has lived or ever will live, and it comes to us through Jesus and through the Holy Spirit in the Church.
- We share in Christ's mission and his power, but we also have to share in his suffering if we are going to share in his glory.
- When Jesus was on the cross, his side was pierced by a lance and blood and water flowed out, symbolizing Baptism (the water) and the Eucharist (the blood). "It was from the side of Christ ... upon the cross that there came forth the 'wondrous sacrament of the whole Church'" (CCC 766).
- We are brought into the Church through the waters of Baptism and sustained by the blood of the Eucharist.

Take It to **Prayer**

Father in heaven, we give you praise, and we thank you so much. We thank you for not giving up on us in our brokenness, for not abandoning us in our weakness. Actually, in our weakness, Lord, you come to us. In our brokenness, you draw close to us. Thank you not only for drawing us close to you. We also thank you for creating a Church where we don't approach you alone. Yes, of course, Lord, we give you our hearts personally and individually. But you also call us to be a family. You call us as brothers and sisters to live in communion with each other and to live in that covenant relationship with you. And so, we ask you to, please, help us to be patient with our brothers and sisters. Help us to be patient with the reality that is the Church. And help us to always live in right relationship with you this day and every day. In Jesus' name, we pray. Amen.

Dive **Deeper**

Since the beginning of time, God had a plan to grow in relationship with you. Spend five minutes in silent meditation thanking God for bringing you into the Church through the water of Baptism, sustained by the blood of the Eucharist.

Reflect on the **Faith**

- Just as Jesus' body is glorified after his death and resurrection, the Church, as the Body of Christ, will ultimately be glorified as well.
- In the Church, we are consoled by the Holy Spirit and healed and fed by the sacraments, but people in the Church sometimes fail us, just as we fail sometimes as followers of Christ.
- God promised that he would bless the world through Abraham and his descendants, and this is fulfilled through Jesus establishing the Church.
- God wants to draw all men to himself, and because of that we have been called to spread his kingdom among all peoples (see CCC 768).
- Just as Jesus was crucified and now his risen body is glorified in heaven for all eternity, the Body of Christ on earth has to experience a similar process of rejection, persecution, and trial before its glorification.
- We live in a broken world, and the Church experiences wounds because of it. At the same time, we have been made for another world, and the Church is filled with the power of the Holy Spirit at every moment to lead us there.

Take It to **Prayer**

Father in heaven, we thank you so much. Thank you for bringing us to this place in time where we get to actually touch eternity. Thank you for bringing us to this Church, where wherever we're standing in the Church, whether we stand in humble submission, whether we stand in love, we stand even in maybe a posture of skepticism or a posture of cynicism, a posture of rebellion ... Lord God, keep us engaged with your Church because I do not want to leave your Body. I don't want to leave the family that you have anointed and established so that you can be known and so that we can be saved. Father, keep us close to your heart, keep us close in your Church, and help us to love one another in ways that we don't yet love. We ask this all in the mighty name of Jesus Christ, our Lord. Amen.

Dive **Deeper**

You are never alone! Our Lord sent the Holy Spirit to be with you in every moment of your life, leading and loving you. Spend time in prayer today reflecting on how the Spirit has guided you in your mission of proclaiming the kingdom of Christ among all peoples this past year.

Reflect on the **Faith**

- In Ephesians 5, St. Paul says, "Christ loved the Church and gave himself up for her, that he might sanctify her, having cleansed her" (Ephesians 5:25–26). We recognize Jesus as the Bridegroom and the Church as his Bride, and to love like Jesus is to love what he loves—in particular, the Church.
- Quoting St. John Paul II, the *Catechism* notes that the Church's "structure is totally ordered to the holiness of Christ's members" (CCC 773). The Church exists for God's love to reach us, and we can respond to it with our love, which is an act of holiness.
- When we receive the sacraments, we come into contact with Christ's mission. The sacraments communicate salvation to us.
- The sacraments are not simply nice symbols, but rather they are the primary instruments through which the Holy Spirit spreads Christ's grace throughout his Church.
- We can easily see the brokenness of the visible Church, and therefore we sometimes miss out on recognizing that it is a vessel of God's love for the whole world as well as a visible sign of the building up of the whole people of God.
- At the Tower of Babel, there was division and a great scattering of humanity, but at Pentecost, the Holy Spirit reunited these people who had been divided.
- We see that the Church is the universal sacrament of salvation because God wants every person to know him fully and be in a relationship both with him and with each other.

Take It to **Prayer**

Father in heaven, we give you praise, and we thank you. We thank you for establishing your Church. We thank you for all that you have done in revealing yourself to Abraham so many years ago, to revealing yourself to the people of God through the voices of the prophets, finally revealing yourself to us fully in your Son. We thank you, and we praise you. We thank you that your Son poured out his Holy Spirit upon the apostles at Pentecost and the birthday of the Church. We thank you that your work, your work in this world, which is the Church—your work has reached our hearts right now. We give you praise and thanks. Please receive our thanks. Receive our praise. And keep us firmly rooted in your heart and rooted in your Church. In Jesus' name, we pray. Amen.

Dive **Deeper**

Challenge yourself to respond to the brokenness of the visible Church with love in an act of holiness as a member of the Body of Christ. Cherish the gift of the sacraments that act as instruments to share Christ's grace throughout his Church.

Reflect on the **Faith**

- God wants us to give our hearts individually to him, but he also wants us to give our hearts to him in communion with our brothers and sisters in faith—as a people, not just individuals.
- We become members of the Church by Baptism. Through Baptism, we are anointed as sons and daughters of God. We are made into a royal priesthood, a prophetic people, and a royal people.
- The Lord called Abraham so that he could build a tribe, people, and nation—ultimately forming a people of faith encompassing the entire world.
- The names we use for the Church are all community-related: the People of God, the Body of Christ, the temple of the Holy Spirit.
- We have a mission to be the salt of the earth and the light of the world, as we have been brought into the mission of Jesus.
- Through the three offices of priest, prophet, and King—by which we are called to imitate Jesus—it is our responsibility to offer sacrifice, declare the Good News, and offer selfless service.

Take It to **Prayer**

Father in heaven, we give you praise and glory. Thank you so much. Thank you for bringing us to this day. Thank you for inviting us to share in your divine life. Thank you for giving us your Holy Spirit, that Spirit of anointing—the Spirit that anointed Jesus Christ, the Anointed One—that priestly, prophetic, and kingly Spirit. We thank you so much, and we ask you to please help us live up to that, help us live up to this high call that you've extended to us this day, today, and every day. In Jesus' name, we pray. Amen.

Dive **Deeper**

You were called to be the "salt of the earth and light of the world" (CCC 782; see Matthew 5:13–16). Who can you serve today in an imitation of Jesus Christ?

Reflect on the **Faith**

- Jesus shared his life intimately with his disciples while he lived on earth, but he promised even more, which is revealed to us after his ascension with the coming of the Holy Spirit (see CCC 787–788).
- The Body of Christ must be unified in the Holy Spirit and our profession of faith in what we believe as Christians.
- We have an intimate relationship with Christ not only because he dwells within us but also because he has given us his own Body and Blood in the Eucharist. So we abide in him in a unique way.
- We place our individuality at the service of the Lord and the Church, but our individuality remains.
- Although virtue and sin can both be personal, neither can be private or isolated from the rest of the Body. Even hidden sin hurts both ourselves and the entire Church, and our virtuous acts, even those that are unknown to many, will bless the Church.

Take It to **Prayer**

Father in heaven, Father, we give you praise. We thank you. We thank you for unity. We thank you for this true oneness. Thank you for extending us not just the teachings of your Son, and not just the salvation of your Son, but thank you for extending to us this union with your Son, this communion with your Son. Thank you for the intimacy that you not only promise but that you bring to us by the gift of your Holy Spirit into our lives. Help us not only to be united more and more fully to your Son, our Lord, help us to be united even more fully with each other. Lord God, we have been made into your Church. Help us to live as your Church. We have been made brothers and sisters. Help us to live as brothers and sisters. We have been made into one Body. Help us to actually be one Body. In Jesus' name, we pray. Amen.

Dive **Deeper**

Ask the Holy Spirit to help reveal your unique, individual gifts. How can you use these gifts in service to the Church and to invite others to share in the promise of the kingdom?

Reflect on the **Faith**

- Idolatry was akin to adultery in the Old Testament; turning away from a covenant relationship with the Lord God was likened to adultery. Looking at Jesus as the Bridegroom and the Church as the Bride, we can more clearly see our call to faithfulness.
- Today, we examine two images: Jesus as the head, and the Church as his Bride.
- In Matthew's Gospel, Jesus is constantly proclaiming that "the kingdom of heaven is at hand" (Matthew 3:2; 4:17).
- We are associated with the suffering as well as the glory of the paschal mystery. We must have the same kind of heart that Jesus does.
- Although as members of Christ's Body we are called to enter his life, death, and resurrection in our own lives, we are not asked to do it alone.
- At the cost of her own life, St. Joan of Arc recognized that even when the Church is broken, the Church is still the Body of Christ and the Bride of Christ (see CCC 795).
- God's calling us into his Church is a call of love, a call to be even more conformed to him as his Body and to allow ourselves to be loved by him as his Bride.

Take It to **Prayer**

Father in heaven, we praise you and give you glory in the name of your Son, Jesus Christ. We ask you to please receive our praise. Receive our thanksgiving. Lord God, hear our prayers. Hear our prayers as a broken body. Hear our prayers as a hurting body. Hear our prayers as your Bride who so often—we have fickle hearts so often. We don't live as your faithful Bride. And yet, you keep calling us back to yourself. You keep being a faithful Bridegroom. You keep being a faithful God and Father, brother, and lover. We thank you so much, God. Thank you so much for loving us and for being faithful even when we are not. Help us to choose you this day and every day of our lives. In Jesus' name, we pray. Amen.

Dive **Deeper**

THE CHURCH, BRIDE OF CHRIST

The resplendent lady pictured has been interpreted as the Blessed Virgin Mary and as the Church, Christ's glorious Bride. Christ the Bridegroom died for the Church, that he might sanctify her and make of her a suitable Bride (see CCC 796).

Reflect on the **Faith**

- The Holy Spirit makes the Church the dwelling place of God, just as he makes each individual Christian a temple of God.
- Charisms help us undertake various tasks and offices for the well-being of the Church (see CCC 799).
- We can think of charisms as "kingdom gifts," which reminds us that they are not for our personal benefit but for the Church.
- Sometimes we are tempted to want the extraordinary gifts, but the Church reminds us to be grateful to the Lord for our own gifts and those of others. St. Paul said, "The eye cannot say to the hand, 'I have no need of you'" (1 Corinthians 12:21). We all need each other.
- Think of the way the world would be changed if every person used the charisms he or she has been given for the glory of God and the service of our brothers and sisters.
- We must discern between what is a genuine spiritual gift and what is not, as well as when is the proper time to use it. We should be docile to the authority of the bishops. (See CCC 801.)

Take It to **Prayer**

Father in heaven, we thank you. We give you praise. We ask you to please receive our prayer. Receive our gratitude. Receive our praise for who you are and what you have done. We ask you to please send your Holy Spirit into our lives. Send your Holy Spirit of unity, your Holy Spirit of sanctity, your Holy Spirit of love, because we know, Lord God, that no matter how many gifts any of us receive, no matter how many gifts any of us exercise, the greatest gift of your Spirit is love. And without love, we are nothing. So pour out your Spirit of love in our hearts so that we can be your love in this world. Help us to say yes to you in this moment and every moment of our lives. In Jesus' name, we pray. Amen.

Dive **Deeper**

What is a charism?

God grants certain special gifts, known as "charisms," to each of us to build up the Church for the salvation of the world. The *Catechism* describes them as either "extraordinary" or "simple and humble" (CCC 799). We notice the extraordinary ones more easily because they are not common: miraculous healing, speaking in tongues, words of prophecy. The more common ones can be overlooked—for example, the graces of administration, faithful service, cheerful care of others, and giving one's time and possessions to those in need.

All of the charisms are *other-directed*—that is, they are intended for the building up of others. All of us are called to serve others in different ways, and the particular charisms allow us to fulfill the responsibilities we have been given in our state of life. For example, God gives priests the charism of preaching and teaching. Because the charisms are other-directed, they call us out of ourselves to love others sacrificially. The *Catechism* asks us to receive our particular gifts with thankfulness and to regulate our use of them according to the single measuring rule of love (see CCC 800).

Key reading: CCC 797–810, 2003–2004

Reflect on the **Faith**

- The Church has been spread to the entire world, and we have inherited it from fishermen and tax collectors.
- There are broken people in the Church, but there is also an unknown multitude of saints. We can easily overlook the fact that a remarkable stream of saints has been raised up by Jesus Christ in his Church over the past two thousand years.
- Many throughout history have tried to destroy the Church, but they have not succeeded. This points to the credibility of the Church's divine nature and mission.
- The Catholic Church is one, holy, catholic, and apostolic; these are the characteristics given by Jesus himself (see CCC 811).
- The Catholic Church can trace every pope back to St. Peter and every bishop to the apostles. We know that they all come from that unbroken line of apostolic succession.
- It is essential that we maintain our unity because the Church is one. Unity is one of the signs of God's presence, while division is a sign of the Evil One.

Take It to **Prayer**

God, we thank you. We thank you, and we praise your name this morning, this afternoon, this evening, whenever we are listening to this, Lord God. We praise you now. And we ask that you please continue to maintain that gift of unity. Lord God, we ask you to please continue to establish your Church in oneness. Lord God, we know that divisions are painful. We know that divisions devastate. And we know the devastation of being divided. We know the devastation of a fracture when the Church fractures or when individuals, members of the Body of Christ, brothers and sisters—when we turn away. So we ask you to please, conquer the sin that divides us. And conquer the sin in each of us that causes division. Knit us back together in our own hearts. Knit us back together with each other as brothers and sisters. And knit us back to you, Father, Son, and Holy Spirit, so that we can be one Body and one Church. In your name we pray. Amen.

Dive **Deeper**

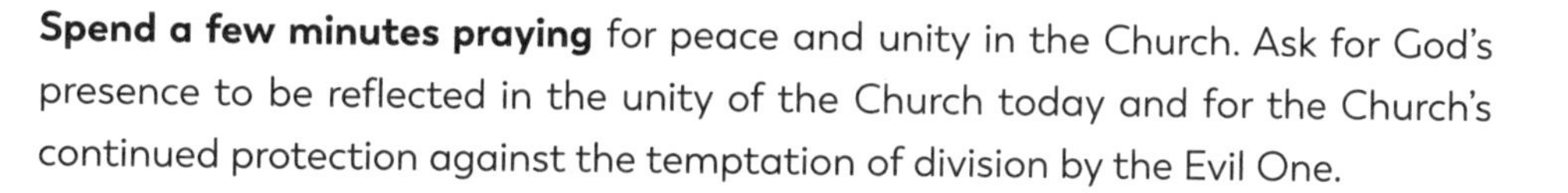

Spend a few minutes praying for peace and unity in the Church. Ask for God's presence to be reflected in the unity of the Church today and for the Church's continued protection against the temptation of division by the Evil One.

Reflect on the **Faith**

- Over the course of our Church's history, there have been significant wounds to our unity that have not healed.
- Sin is what causes division among us. At the Last Supper, Jesus begs his Father that his followers may all be one.
- We should never be content with division in the Body of Christ when Jesus specifically prayed for us to be united. This should cause us great pain; if we love what Jesus loves, then we should love unity and be hurt by its absence.
- Many of our non-Catholic brothers and sisters in Christ love the Word of God. We received this Word, the Scriptures, through the Church, through the discernment the Holy Spirit gave to the apostles and their successors.
- The truth of the Catholic Church is a gift. Like St. Paul, we should not boast in anything except for the cross of Jesus Christ (see Galatians 6:14).
- Jesus prays for unity at the Last Supper, and we must pray and strive for the unity of all Christians. That is a gift of Christ and a call of the Holy Spirit.

Take It to **Prayer**

Father in heaven, we give you praise. And we call upon your Holy Spirit, the Holy Spirit that is the soul of the Church. Lord God, we, followers of Christ, your Son—we experience division. Not only do we experience division in our own hearts and division in our relationships, but there are divisions among your believers, and you don't want them. You don't rejoice in those things. You don't rejoice in those divisions. They grieve your heart. And so we ask you, Lord, help bring us back together because it is not the action of human beings that will ever bring the Church back together. It will only be the work of grace. It will only be your work that brings your Body back into one, that heals the divisions among all Christians. It will only be your grace and your miracle that can take your Body that has been so torn and tattered and battered and make it whole again. But we know that you can do this, Lord. Even in spite of our brokenness, in spite of our sin, we know you can work that miracle. So we ask you, Lord God, this day, work that miracle, overcome what divides us by what unites us. And make us one again for your glory and so that the world may know that you have sent your Son, Jesus Christ. We make this prayer in his name. Amen.

Dive **Deeper**

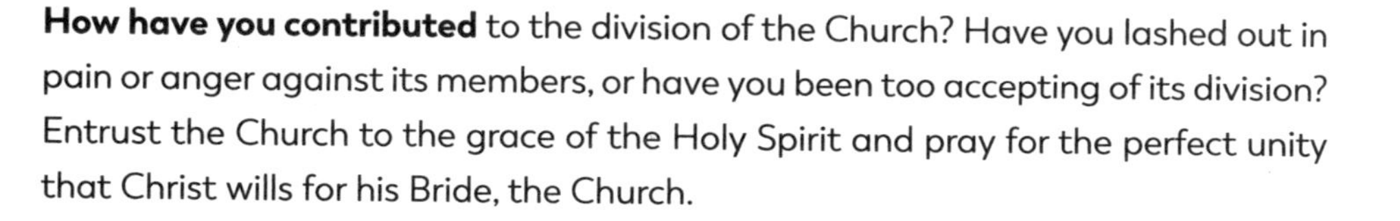

How have you contributed to the division of the Church? Have you lashed out in pain or anger against its members, or have you been too accepting of its division? Entrust the Church to the grace of the Holy Spirit and pray for the perfect unity that Christ wills for his Bride, the Church.

Reflect on the **Faith**

- "The Church ... is held, as a matter of faith, to be unfailingly holy. This is because Christ, the Son of God, who with the Father and the Spirit is hailed as 'alone holy,'" made her holy (CCC 823). Therefore, this is what we believe.
- God is the one who makes the Church holy (see CCC 824).
- What is all the work of the Church oriented toward? It is all for "the sanctification of men in Christ and the glorification of God" (CCC 824).
- This is a call to keep going, continuing to repent and recognize that we are sinners. In the parable of the weeds and the wheat (Matthew 13:24–30), we recognize that God himself has planted good seed, but there is also sin, even in our own hearts. And so we ask the Lord to continue to purify us. (See CCC 827.)
- The saints are saints because they loved and did what God asked of them. They had heroic virtue, and they lived by the Holy Spirit in holiness.
- Love is more than affection—it must be effective and move us to do works of love, to love God with everything we have and to love our neighbor as ourself.

Take It to **Prayer**

Father in heaven, thank you. Thank you for being the source of holiness. Thank you for being you, Lord God. We praise you and we give you thanks, that you are the only thrice-holy God. You're the only one who is holy, holy, holy, Lord. So we lift up your name, and we praise you this day. We thank you for the gift of your Church. We thank you for the gift of your Holy Spirit. We thank you that you have never, ever given up on us and that you have declared you never, ever will give up on us. We ask you to please help us to not give up on you. Help us to not stop choosing you. Lord God, we ask you to please send your Holy Spirit into every area of challenge in our lives so that we can face every challenge with your strength. In Jesus' name we pray. Amen.

Dive **Deeper**

The sacrament of Reconciliation can often be intimidating, especially if you have not gone for a while. Take some time today to pray through an examination of conscience, acknowledging your sinfulness, and make a plan to go to confession. Remain steadfast in your desire to pursue the Holy Spirit's gift of holiness and grow in virtue.

Reflect on the **Faith**

- "'Catholic' means 'universal,'" and the Church is catholic because Christ is the universal means of salvation for the entire world (see CCC 830–831).
- Knowing the fullness of the Church requires a "correct and complete confession of faith" and a "full sacramental life" (CCC 830). We ought to know the fullness of the one we love most.
- There are wounds to the unity of the Church through sin. It is not good that the Church is divided.
- The Church Fathers profess the union that all the "particular churches" have to have with the Church in Rome (CCC 834).
- There is no background, temptation, sin, or history of brokenness that excludes anyone from God's embrace. "All men are called to this catholic unity of the People of God" (CCC 836). It is for everyone.
- Being Catholic means accepting the Faith, worshipping the same way as the Church does with all the sacraments, acknowledging the role of the hierarchy and governing order in the Church, and accepting the Pope and the bishops. If we reject some things we do not like, we are not continuing in love. And if we do not continue in love, we are not saved. This is important.
- God longs for us to say yes to him fully in all that he has revealed about himself.

Take It to **Prayer**

Father in heaven, we thank you. We thank you and give you praise. We thank you for the gift of faith and hope and love. We ask you to please increase our faith, so that we can trust you all the more—not only trust what you have done, but also trust what you are doing. Give us hope, not only to belong to you today, but to belong to you in the future. And give us love, the love that will never end, love that will last, and endure, and be alive forever in heaven. Lord God, we ask you to give us these incredible gifts of faith, hope, and love. Keep us deeply rooted in you, in your heart. Keep us deeply rooted in your Church. We make this prayer in the mighty name of Jesus Christ, our Lord. Amen.

Dive **Deeper**

Reflect on your role as a member of the Body of Christ in the Catholic Church. How can you help repair the Church's wounds against unity and bring others into the fullness of revelation?

Reflect on the **Faith**

- Today we are looking at what the Church's relationship is with religions around the world. We realize the Church does not give herself gifts; she has been given them by the Lord himself. It is our duty, our privilege, and our responsibility to exercise them and to understand what this means.
- Jesus comes from the Jewish people, so we are closely related to them (see CCC 839).
- Because of original sin, all of us are fallen, so we recognize that we need the Church and her fullness of truth.
- As written in *Lumen Gentium*, "Basing itself on Scripture and Tradition, the Council teaches that the Church, a pilgrim now on Earth, is necessary for salvation" (CCC 846).
- Jesus says, "I am the way, and the truth, and the life; no one comes to the Father, but by me" (John 14:6).
- The grace of Christ of salvation comes to us through his Body, the Church, so to reject this grace is to reject him.
- "Those who, through no fault of their own, do not know the Gospel of Christ or his Church, but who nevertheless seek God with a sincere heart, and, moved by grace, try in their actions to do his will as they know it through the dictates of their conscience—those too may achieve eternal salvation" (CCC 847).
- We must bring the Gospel to every part of the world.

Take It to **Prayer**

Father in heaven, we thank you, and we give you praise. We ask you to, please, enlighten our minds. Help us to understand clearly exactly what it is you wish to reveal to us not only about yourself, your heart, your love, who you are, but also about your Church. Your Son, Jesus Christ, is the head of the Church. And the Church is the Body of Christ. We ask you, Lord, help us to actually live united with our head. Help us live in union with your will. Help us to always see ourselves as constantly in need of reformation and at the same time constantly being given your grace. Help us to acknowledge the goodness that we find in every person and all peoples around us. Help us find the goodness and the truth that we find in varying degrees in all religions. Help us to acknowledge the dignity of every human being, our brothers and our sisters who are close to us and those people who are strangers, who are far away from us. Help us to acknowledge and express the dignity that they have inherited by being made in your image. Help us to love everyone, especially those closest to us. And we ask this in the name of Jesus Christ, our Lord. Amen.

Dive **Deeper**

Why does the Church say that "salvation is through the Church"?

This is an invitation to those who do not know or understand the great gift of the Church. The Catholic Church is a "sign of contradiction" to the world, teaching the revealed truths of the Faith. The eternal Son of God, Jesus Christ, became man to save us from sin and to show us exactly how to love. Jesus is the only Savior. He established his Church on earth to spread the Gospel so all people can come to know God, receive his grace through the gift of the sacraments, and spend eternity with him in heaven. To those outside the Church, we can stand as witnesses to the Gospel, inviting them to experience her gifts. We can pray for them, commending them to God's great mercy—as we ask for his mercy on us.

Further Reading: Second Vatican Council, "Declaration on the Relation of the Church to Non-Christian Religions" (*Nostra Aetate*); Roch A. Kereszty, O. Cist., *Christianity Among Other Religions: Apologetics in a Contemporary Context*, ed. Andrew C. Gregg; St. Justin Martyr, *Dialogue with Trypho*, 45; Second Vatican Council, *Lumen Gentium*, 16; St. John Paul II, encyclical letter *Redemptoris Missio*, 10, 18; Congregation for the Doctrine of the Faith, *Dominus Iesus*, August 6, 2000

Reflect on the **Faith**

- We are saved only by Jesus Christ.
- If we are not living on mission, then we are not actually disciples of Jesus. So the Church must be missionary. (See CCC 849.)
- Christ's final word to the apostles is called the Great Commission, indicating that we are commanded to go on mission.
- There are people living in the world who have no idea that God exists and how much he knows and loves them, and God desires us to help bring them to him so they can receive salvation.
- The martyrs who bore witness to the Gospel appeared to be destroyed, but what looked like weakness became fruitful.
- Every human being is made for love yet has a broken heart. So we can be tempted to run away from truth.

Take It to **Prayer**

Father in heaven, we know that you have met us with your grace. We know that you have given us your Holy Spirit. We know that you have sent your Son into this world to be our Savior. He becomes our brother. He is our God. You have used other people in our lives to bring us this knowledge of truth. There are people in our lives who have given so much that we could know the truth. Lord God, we ask you to give us a missionary spirit. Give us the same Spirit that lived in those people who brought us the Gospel. Give us a heart for others; give us a faithfulness and a contagious teachability. Give us availability so that we can be sent on mission, we can bring your truth, your Word, and your grace to a world that longs for you even if they don't know it. In Jesus' name, we pray. Amen.

Dive **Deeper**

ST. PAUL IN ATHENS

St. Paul understood well the Church's missionary mandate. Here we see the "apostle to the Gentiles" preaching in Athens. The apostles helped to spread the message of Christ and his salvation to the ends of the earth (see CCC 849).

Reflect on the **Faith**

- The Church has many invisible realities but also those which are visible, including the historical fact that Jesus called these twelve men to be the first bishops.
- This is not just a thing of the past. Jesus gives the apostles' successors that same authority.
- One of the greatest reasons to join the Catholic Church is its unbroken line of apostolic succession all the way back to Jesus, who commissioned his apostles to go forth and then ordain others to serve after them.
- In the book of Revelation, John sees the new Jerusalem, and it is built on the twelve apostles (see Revelation 21). "Christ promised to remain with them always. The divine mission entrusted by Jesus to them 'will continue to the end of time'" (CCC 860).
- Jesus said, "He who receives you receives me" (Matthew 10:40; see CCC 858). If we reject those he has sent, then we are rejecting him. In this, the Lord is calling us to grow more and more in love for him.
- It is a gift to know what it means that the Church is one, holy, Catholic, and apostolic.

Take It to **Prayer**

Father in heaven, thank you so much. Thank you for bringing us to this day. Thank you for bringing us to day 120. We thank you for continuing to guide the Church that you built on the foundation stones of the apostles. Thank you for giving us their successors. Thank you for continuing to sanctify your Church. Thank you for continuing to guide your Church. Thank you for continuing to guard your Church. We ask that those who are our bishops right now—we ask you to protect them. We ask you to inspire them. We ask you to purify their hearts so that they can be men after your own heart, so that they can lead well, they can shepherd well, they can govern well. Lord God, we pray in this moment for any shepherd in your Church who stands in particular need of your grace, who stands in particular need of your help in this moment. And I want to just give us all a chance even to name our own bishop, to name our local bishop, just we pray for him now. Pray for your bishop right now. In this moment, we just lift him up before you, Father. I pray for my bishop, Daniel. I pray that you continue to guide and guard, to lead him, so that he can guide and guard and lead all of us. Make them all great fathers. We ask you this, Father, in the name of your Son, Jesus Christ, our Lord. Amen.

Dive **Deeper**

Think of someone in your life who is not in communion with the fullness of the Catholic Church. Pray for a renewal of his or her faith and acceptance into the full sacramental life found in our one, holy, catholic, and apostolic church.

CONCLUDING SUMMARY

This first part of the *Catechism* has the overarching intention of making accessible and understandable for us the love of the one true God, who is Father, Son, and Holy Spirit. Every aspect of the Church's teaching points to the truth of who God is and what he intends for his creation. Our response to God's gift of himself in Jesus Christ is faith. As the Bride longed for by the divine Bridegroom, the Church responds in faith, calling all of its members to entrust themselves wholeheartedly to him.

CONCLUDING QUESTIONS AND ANSWERS

1. **Does everyone have a desire for God?**

   Yes. But this desire can be forgotten, overlooked, or rejected. It manifests itself in the universal search for truth and happiness (see CCC 27–29).

2. **Can we know with certainty the existence of a personal God?**

   Yes. Everyone can come to know that there is a personal God from the evidence of the human person and of the world. But our struggles with sin and difficulties in our environment and upbringing can make this knowledge difficult to reach (CCC 31–38).

3. **Who wrote Sacred Scripture?**

   Various human authors, whose writing was inspired by God, who is the "primary Author" of Scripture (see CCC 105–106).

4. **Who are the two great biblical models of faith offered to us in the *Catechism*?**

   Abraham and Mary (see CCC 144–149).

5. **How many articles are there in the Apostles' Creed?**

   Twelve. This shows the fullness of faith symbolized by the number of apostles (see CCC 191).

6. **What are the implications of our faith in the one true God?**

   We recognize God's greatness and majesty; live in thanksgiving; know the unity and dignity of all people, created in God's image; make good use of his creation; and trust him in every situation and circumstance (see CCC 222–227).

7. What is the central mystery of Christian faith and life?

The Holy Trinity. This is the essential reality and truth at the heart of everything we believe and do (see CCC 234).

8. Is God male?

No. "God transcends the human distinction between the sexes." That said, Jesus prays to his "Father" and commands us to do so, and Jesus became incarnate as a man. As the *Catechism* states, "No one is father as God is Father" (CCC 239).

9. What is the term the Church uses to describe all of the actions by which God protects and governs the journey of his creation to its ultimate perfection?

Divine Providence (CCC 302).

10. Is it right to describe our life as a battle?

Yes. The whole of history is a battle with the powers of evil. But it is a battle we can be confident Christ has won, and he will give us a share in his victory if we trust him (see CCC 407–412).

11. Can we rightly say things such as, "One of the Trinity lived in Nazareth," "God got into a boat, or "God suffered on the cross"?

Yes. The Council of Constantinople said that "everything in Christ's human nature is to be attributed to his divine person." What we always mean is, "God, in the human nature he assumed, lived in Nazareth, got into a boat, suffered on the Cross," and so on (see CCC 468).

12. Who was responsible for Jesus' death?

Ultimately, all sinners are responsible (see CCC 598).

13. After his death, did Jesus descend into the hell of the damned?

No. “He descended into hell” means he descended into the realm of the dead, of all those who had died before he came (see CCC 632–635).

14. Who were the first to find the tomb empty?

The holy women (CCC 640).

15. What are the main symbols of the Holy Spirit in the Scriptures?

Water, anointing, fire, cloud and light, the seal, the hand, the finger, the dove (see CCC 694–701).

16. What does “Christus totus” mean?

The “whole Christ”—Jesus Christ and his Church, the head and his members (CCC 795).

17. What are the four “marks” of the Church mentioned in the Creed?

One, holy, catholic, and apostolic.

NOTES

1. C. S. Lewis, *Mere Christianity* (New York: HarperOne, 2001), 136–137.
2. John Paul II, *Redemptoris Missio* (December 7, 1990), 39, vatican.va.
3. C. S. Lewis, *The Great Divorce* (New York: HarperOne, 2001), 69.
4. John Paul II, *Ecclesia in America* (January 22, 1999), 17, vatican.va.
5. "Truth Cannot Contradict Truth," address of St. John Paul II to the Pontifical Academy of Sciences, 2, October 22, 1996, newadvent.org.
6. "Truth Cannot Contradict Truth," 6.
7. "In You, O Woman Full of Grace," quoted in "Singing the Anaphora of St. Basil the Great," Metropolitan Cantor Institute (website), The Byzantine Catholic Archeparchy of Pittsburgh, accessed June 16, 2023, mci.archpitt.org.
8. Rick Warren, *The Purpose Driven Life* (Grand Rapids, MI: Zondervan, 2012), 262.